Strategic Research and Political Communications for NGOs

Strategic Research and Political Communications for NGOs

Initiating Policy Change

Accenture-Stiftung, Germany
School of Communication Management,
International University in Germany, Bruchsal
The Banyan, India

Los Angeles | London | New Delhi
Singapore | Washington DC | Melbourne

First published in 2009 by

 SAGE Publications India Pvt Ltd
B1/I-1 Mohan Cooperative Industrial Area
Mathura Road, New Delhi 110 044, India
www.sagepub.in

SAGE Publications Inc
2455 Teller Road
Thousand Oaks, California 91320, USA

SAGE Publications Ltd
1 Oliver's Yard, 55 City Road
London EC1Y 1SP, United Kingdom

SAGE Publications Asia-Pacific Pte Ltd
3 Church Street
#10-04 Samsung Hub
Singapore 049483

Published by Vivek Mehra for SAGE Publications India Pvt Ltd, typeset in 10/13pt Book Antiqua by Star Compugraphics Private Limited, Delhi.

Library of Congress Cataloging-in-Publication Data

Strategic research and political communications for NGOs: initiating policy change/Accenture-Stiftung, Germany, School of Communication Management, International University in Germany, Bruchsal, The Banyan, India.

    p. cm.

Includes bibliographical references.

    1. Non-governmental organizations. 2. Strategic planning. 3. Social advocacy. 4. Bruchsal (Germany) I. Accenture-Stiftung (Germany) II. International University in Germany. School of Communication Management. III. Banyan (Organization)

JZ4841.S77	659.2 – dc22	2009	2009027296

ISBN: 978-81-321-0120-8 (PB)

The SAGE Team: Elina Majumdar, Jayshree Kewalramani, Vijay Sah and Trinankur Banerjee

Contents

List of Tables

List of Figures

Preface

THE NGOS VIEW: VANDANA GOPIKUMAR AND VAISHNAVI JAYAKUMAR (THE BANYAN, INDIA)

Vandana Gopikumar and Vaishnavi Jayakumar are the Founders and Managing Trustees of The Banyan, India

THIS PUBLICATION aims to add value to the work being done by non-governmental organizations and social entrepreneurs. While the references are broadly global, the focus is on the Indian development scenario. Being entrepreneurs in the social sector ourselves, we realized the importance of this initiative and welcomed the partnership with the Accenture-Stiftung, Germany and the International University in Germany, Bruchsal.

Our work at The Banyan, has opened our eyes to the problems that plague not just the mental health space, but society at large. In a country like India, most issues are often interlinked and the bottom line is the need to address larger issues such as the social and rural/urban divide. With a large percentage of the population clearly below the poverty line, the lack of basic amenities such as access to health, housing, education, water and food pose serious problems and shadow almost every issue the social sector faces. While the government and corporations play a significant role in funding, strategizing and implementing interventions, the role of the NGO sector is critical and perhaps has scope to ensure maximum impact. However, most often, skilled, committed and socially charged and inclined individuals who run such organizations are bogged down with day-to-day interventions and sometimes lose focus of the larger issue. Being hard-core practitioners ourselves, several times providing food, clothing and treatment took precedence over scientifically evaluating our impact, assessing gaps or creating a strategic game plan to combat the problem in its entirety. It is only after almost 11 years into our work, that concepts such as scalability, replicability, standardization and advocacy to initiate policy change took a clear, structured form. Not to say that they didn't exist earlier, they did, but more in the mind and at a subconscious level.

Social work education and the profession itself need to be revamped a little and can do with some brand building. Despite the scope of a social worker ranging from a case and group worker to a development strategist, exposure to some of the best practices documented in this book are far from being passed on early in one's career.

This book aims to bridge the gap between the need to dive in and intervene to make a difference, and the need to explore high impact strategic solutions to core problems that haunt our society. Several of the principles, strategies, theories and methodologies spoken about in the book coupled with good examples from national and international implementing and activist organizations provide sound background and information on professional social and development work. The book clearly focuses on the technical skills required as a social entrepreneur.

Learning is an ongoing process and most of this is usually on the job. However, a precise and rounded piece of information such as this can certainly kick start the process of professionalizing the social sector and on working towards more sustainable models of social intervention. With the current concept of the public–private partnerships working well and yielding good results in most spheres, the NGO world clearly has a lot to achieve; and how better to achieve this than to have both a passionate and a prepared studied and smart approach.

THE CORPORATE FOUNDATION'S VIEW: DR STEPHAN SCHOLTISSEK (ACCENTURE-STIFTUNG)

Dr Stephan Scholtissek is Accenture's Geographic Unit Managing Director for Austria, Switzerland and Germany and Chairman of the Accenture–Stiftung, Germany

The Accenture–Stiftung (Foundation) is really excited about this project. We believe that collaboration, knowledge exchange and synergies among different spaces of the economy will result in better results for everyone. Exploring ways on how to apply and share the methodologies and tools used in the profit, non-profit and academic world is a worthwhile exercise.

Our foundation has two main objectives, one of them being education. We also focus on people in need. This book combines our two main goals, providing an academic approach on how to professionally address and change the situation of people in need.

In our role as a global organization, Accenture believes we have a responsibility to engage proactively with the communities in which we live and work. Globally, the Accenture Foundation spends more than $6 million for charitable causes per annum. We are active in over 30 countries, focusing on projects that affect livelihoods with measurable outcomes and an accent on long-term sustainability.

Being a global player with a presence in over 50 countries has taught us that issues and challenges can't be addressed or resolved within the borders of a single country. We are delighted that this project will contribute to close the gap.

THE ACADEMIC VIEW: DR SVENJA FALK (ACCENTURE-STIFTUNG) AND PROFESSOR ANDREA RÖMMELE (INTERNATIONAL UNIVERSITY IN GERMANY, BRUCHSAL)

Dr Svenja Falk leads Accenture Research in Asia Pacific. She is Visiting Professor at the International University in Germany, Bruchsal and a member of the Advisory Board of the Accenture-Stiftung.

Professor Andrea Römmele holds the chair of Communication Management at the International University in Germany, Bruchsal. She is the Director of the BA in International Communication Management at the International University in Germany, Bruchsal.

This project is the launch pad of a series looking at the intersection of business, academia and the media from an international perspective. We believe that this project would help better understand the dynamics and governance of globalization. Many studies have looked at the economic, political and cultural implications of this 'tectonic shift', focusing on showing evidence for the fact itself. Whether it is the 'flat' or 'multipolar', the 'one' or more 'antagonistic' world, the question of governance remains under-exposed. However, it is obvious that the amount of stakeholders around specific policy questions have increased — governance among a network of complex interest groups rather than authorized government decisions is going to be the fundament of how we 'do things' in the future.

We both serve as spokeswomen for a group on 'Political Consulting' under the umbrella of the German Association for Political Science. In a number of publications and conferences we have addressed the topic of the intersection from a German perspective. We are excited to take it to the next more international level, starting with this book.

Acknowledgements

THIS BOOK is the outcome of an exciting collaboration among a corporate foundation, an NGO and a university. The authors Accenture–Stiftung (Kronberg), School of Communication Management, International University in Germany (Bruchsal) and The Banyan (Chennai) would like to thank Andrea Römmele and Svenja Falk for their support in making this book happen.

A number of people from The Banyan and The Banyan Academy of Leadership in Mental Health have been helping to give shape and form to this project. To name only a few out of the incredibly supportive team: Vandana Gopikumar and Vaishnavi Jayakumar, the two founders of The Banyan, and Madhuri Menon, Madhu Sharan, Bettina Müller and Valentin Fliess.

Sarah Bastgen's contribution to the book cannot be over-emphasized. She travelled to India from Bruchsal to do the fieldwork in cooperation with the NGOs on site. Besides providing valuable inputs to the research, she also formulated the case studies. Her commitment made a real difference to the project.

We would particularly like to thank the NGOs profiled in the book for their kind support, responsiveness and valuable contributions. Their openness to spending time and sharing information with us has been outstanding!

We would also like to thank Dr Sugata Ghosh, Vice President, Commissioning at Sage Publications for his sponsorship and support. Elina Majumdar, Commissioning Editor, has been outstanding in her commitment to this project.

Svenja Falk would like to thank Balraj Vasudevan for initiating the Bangalore meeting in 2007 where the idea for the book was born; Frank Funicello for the rigour in attacking her *alemanol*;

Charlotte Raut for providing insights into survey research; Kai Hitz and Mattias Wahrendorff for their support with insights and graphs; and the students of International University in Germany, Bruchsal for providing the background research. And last but not the least is her debt to daughter Ana Carina who, in trying times, has been and continues to be her unfailing source of joy, happiness and strength.

Introduction

THIS BOOK was initiated and completed in a space that marked the intersection of academia, business and the non-profit world. We believe that the methods, experiences and different approaches to thinking of these three domains can help create synergies resulting in higher levels of innovation. As our primary research shows, NGOs can be considered as creative, flexible and innovative in their approaches to pursue innovative business models, political communication and stakeholder management. Furthermore, companies can learn a lot on the subject of employee motivation and loyalty from the non-profit sector, which continues to be able to provide a differentiating value proposition to many employees. NGOs can learn from operational excellence of companies in running their business, especially when it comes to adapting to changing market conditions. Academia can provide the tools and frameworks for assessing and evaluating outcomes and act as a moderator between worlds. Academia wants to maximize knowledge, corporations are thriving to maximize revenue and NGOs are keen to initiate policy change to maximize opportunity and equality for their constituents. Policy change results in different approaches when making laws and regulations, distributing resources and making other decisions that affect peoples' lives. The principal aim of initiating policy change is that decision makers create reform policies and ensure that those policies are implemented.

We are not only undertaking this task in a context of the intersection of these three societal spheres, but have also decided to look at it from the perspective of India. India has been one of the most stunning examples of a third world country changing to become one of the fastest growing emerging markets and now inevitably on its way to becoming a global political and economic powerhouse. We believe that India will look completely different 10 years from now. We are convinced that the non-profit sector — already strong today — will play a critical role in securing inclusive growth and equality. Synergies among academia, business and NGOs could be one key enabler, and India can set an example for other countries by being at the fore of those taking the same path to modernization.

In this book, we shall familiarize the reader with the tools and methods to develop a strategy and communicate it accordingly, thus making the world a better place. We introduce NGOs that have developed best practices in strategy formulation and communication to provide structured, hands-on evidence of how one can really make a structural difference. We start by describing a little about the non-profit sector in general and about communication as being one prerequisite for successfully positioning a topic on the public agenda so as to get support for approaching it differently and, ideally, changing the way a society goes about its approach. We present the specifics of the NGO sector in India, its history, the size of the sector in various policy fields and the financial spend. Also, we briefly look at the differences among the US, Europe and Asia when it comes to the non-profit sector and its communication systems.

We then introduce a framework for initiating policy change. Every step which is needed is explained and strategic tools are introduced so the change can be actually performed. The book contains best practice examples of NGOs from across the globe which are actually doing this particularly well. Our findings are supported by a set of case studies based on primary interviews and illustrated in the last part of the book.

Chapter One

NGOs on the Agenda—Profile of an Agent Provocateur

NUMEROUS NON-GOVERNMENTAL organizations (NGOs) or not-for-profit organizations (NPOs) were established with the objective of influencing policy decisions and shaping political perspectives on issues ranging from humanitarian law to environmental protection. Their main reason for being is to initiate policy change to make the ecosystem in a specific policy field better. Across the globe, they are key influencers in policy formulation and change.

NGOs have emerged in many shapes and forms: as associations, foundations or non-commercial entities. Regardless of national origin or social cause, they do not operate to optimize profits or shareholder value but to increase the quality of life and dignity for every citizen. According to the UN Department of Public Information (DPI) website, an NGO is a not-for-profit, voluntary citizens' group, which is organized on a local, national or international level so as to address issues in support of the public good. Policy-oriented and made up of people with shared interests, NGOs perform a variety of services and humanitarian functions, bring citizens' concerns to governments, monitor public policy and program implementation and encourage participation of civil society at the community level. They provide analysis and expertise, apply early warning mechanisms and help monitor and implement national and international agreements. Often, they influence policy formulation right from the beginning through to being part of a commission of experts participating in parliamentary or juridical hearings.

Human rights NGOs such as Amnesty International, Human Rights Watch and the Ford Foundation have become the most powerful and well-funded members of this large community — more than once they have put governments across the globe in uncomfortable situations through their permanent and sometimes aggressive campaigning aimed at alerting the public and raising awareness. On the trans-national level, so-called NGO-Multis like Amnesty International or Greenpeace have become important agents in driving the agenda in certain policy fields. On the national level, foundations like the Bertelsmann Foundation in Germany or the Rockefeller Foundation in the US have significantly influenced policy formulation on both a state and trans-national level.

NGOs mobilize political action and agenda setting, participate in decision-making, carefully monitor the performance of governments and corporations, and publicize their judgments. 'Since they are not powerful in a traditional sense of the word, they must use the power of their information, ideas, and strategies to alter the information and value contexts within which states make policies' (Keck and Sikkink 1998: 16). Often, they are the voice of choice in the media as they provide an alternative perspective on issues.

TYPOLOGY OF NGOs

Ever since the emergence of the concept of private voluntary organizations as an important voice on the international landscape, with the objective of revitalizing civil society, various types and forms of these organizations have come into existence:

1. INGO: International NGOs such as Médecins Sans Frontières. These NGOs function or have membership across at least two countries without primary loyalty, identification or reliance on a national government; thus they exist as entities beyond nation-states (Cooprrider and Pasmore 1991: 1042).
2. BINGO: Business Orientated International NGO, like the International Labour Organization (ILO) or ISACA, formerly known as the Information Systems Audit and Control Association, specific to IT governance and security.

3. ENGO: Environmental NGOs. Examples are World Wildlife Fund (WWF), Friends of the Earth, Greenpeace, and Robin Wood.

4. GINGO: For example Amnesty International, Genuine NGOs which consist only of individuals and are funded 100 per cent by membership fees (Voss 2007: 26).

5. GONGO: Government operated NGOs, mainly paid through governments, like the International Committee of the Red Cross (Furtak 1997: 25).

6. QUANGOs: Quasi-Autonomous Non-Governmental Organizations which also allow membership to states and often rely on governmental aid. Examples are the International Organization for Standardization (ISO), the International Union for the Conservation of Nature (IUCN).

7. Networks: Network of NGOs from various policy fields pursuing a specific cause. One example is the NGO Ban Landmines, a network of 1400 NGOs from 90 countries.

8. Social Movements: Social movements lack the degree of institutionalization of an organization. They are informal groupings of individuals geared towards change in society. One of the most famous social movements of the 20th century is the American Civil Rights movement in the United States or the Green movement in Europe. Very often, social movements evolve into institutions; the Green movement, for example, resulted in the foundation of political parties (Tilly 2004).

According to the typology of the World Bank and the Asian Development Bank, NGOs can be classified as either operational or advocacy. Operational NGOs like the International Committee of the Red Cross or Caritas 'get a job done' through the design and implementation of a development-related project and contribution or delivery of welfare services, including emergency relief and environmental protection and management. Areas might be disaster relief or infrastructure improvements such as the installation of water purification systems. An advocacy NGO promotes change for a specific cause. These are principally concerned with normative matters aimed at setting norms and policy seeking (Gordenker and

Weiss 1996: 42). The main objective of their work is to raise public awareness about specific problems through activist events, public relation activities and lobbying. Advocacy NGOs strive to bring a social, economic or environment-related deficiency to public attention to push for the implementation of certain standards and, in the longer run, to initiate policy change. One might even say that a successful NGO in this arena makes itself redundant, as – hopefully – the cause for their existence will have successfully been eliminated through policy change. We often find NGOs which start as operational NGOs and then increase focus on advocacy as they mature and grow.

In this book, we focus on advocacy NGOs, understanding well that we are facing an overlap with interest groups (for example automobile associations) as well as foundations, which often have one major source of funding in a political party or a company, and which sometimes considerably influence their areas of interest and messaging.

Mostly, trans-national organizations are equipped with sufficient financial means and expert clusters to professionally raise awareness for issues in their specific policy field. Through their formal and informal networks they are linked around the world and therefore have larger access to funding, skills and knowledge. Their operations are often professionalized and structured; they perceive themselves as professional social entrepreneurs rather than social activists. They are the white collar workers of the non-profits and their main arenas are the conference room, the university auditorium or the CEO suite and they appear in public raising voice for a specific issue. They are literate in interacting with the media and decision makers based on a very good understanding of the inner workings of a society. One successful example would be Room to Read, a US based NGO which partners with local communities throughout the developing world to establish schools, libraries and other educational infrastructure.

However, organizations operating within one country – often at the grassroots level – normally have to manage on smaller budgets and are less well-connected to expert groups to raise their knowledge base. One example would be Carpus e.V., a small Germany-based NGO dealing with development assistance and resource protection in the Philippines. Carpus e.V. aims at supporting local Philippine NGOs to preserve natural resources and to build a sustained civil society in this region.

THE ROLE OF NGOs

NGOs are widely recognized as one of the key players in setting agendas in communities and states. With the creeping retreat of the state from welfare in the mature economies, NGOs as well as businesses play a central role in securing a healthy and inclusive environment for citizens worldwide. In the developing countries, especially in the emerging markets, NGOs can be seen as critical agents in addressing the social costs of rapid modernization, and ensuring that the benefits and costs are spread equally across the population. Many social and economic issues are trans-national in nature and cannot be resolved within the borders of a nation–state. Here and there, NGOs are seen as providing the nucleus of a civil society (Nathan et al. 2008). While NGOs serve a variety of causes, a cardinal principle is that they operate according to their missions and often refer to the so-called 'good cause'. Nevertheless they act in a manner consistent with the objectives for which they receive funds. Donations are an NGO's lifeline because by definition they are independent organizations. Even though the term 'non-governmental organization' implies independence from governments, some NGOs rely heavily on governments for their grants. Ban Landmines, for example, a network of 1,400 NGOs in 90 countries headquartered in Washington, DC is almost entirely funded through governments. Funding can also come from national governments, the EU, the UN or other inter-national bodies, as well as private trusts and philanthropies, re-ligious institutions, individual donations and other NGOs. There is a wide variety of NGOs or NPOs that take the legal form of an asso-ciation, a society or club depending on the legislative framework of the country of residence. However, many of them do not register officially at all, resulting in a challenge to quantify the number of NGOs in a certain country or, indeed, globally.

Size of the NGO Sector

It is true that there are some sources quantifying the NGO sector by country or globally. However, because different criteria are used to assess the numbers, the size of the sector can vary significantly and can only be used as indicative.

There are three main sources assessing international NGOs.

1. The United Nations (UN). The UN grants consultative status to NGOs which meet the criteria of official registration with the appropriate government authorities as an NGO or NPO for at least two years, which must have an established headquarters as well as a democratically adopted constitution, which has the authority to speak for its members, which has a representative structure and appropriate mechanisms of accountability, and which practices democratic and transparent decision-making processes. Furthermore, their basic resources must be derived mainly from contributions of the national affiliates or other components or from individual members. In July 2007, 3,172 NGOs worldwide had consultative status with the Economic and Social Council (ECOSOC).

2. The Union of International Associations (UIA). In order to define a non-governmental organization, this international association has established a number of criteria around objectives, structure, governance and activities. According to UIA, there were 68,868 international NGOs globally in 2006 (UIA 2007). They have defined a set of criteria which an NGO should meet to be recognized by the organization:

    (a) The goals must be genuinely international in character, with the intention to cover operations in at least three countries. Hence bodies such as the International Action Committee for Safeguarding the Nubian Monuments or the Anglo-Swedish Society are excluded. Societies devoted solely to commemorating particular individuals are likewise ineligible, even if they have made major contributions to the international community.

(b) There must be individual or collective participation of the members, with full voting rights, from at least three countries. Membership must be open to any appropriately qualified individual or entity in the organization's area of operations. Closed groups are therefore excluded, although the situation becomes ambiguous when only one member is allowed per country by the organization, thus effectively closing the organization to other qualified groups in that country. Voting power must be such that no one national group can control the organization. National organizations which accept foreigners as members are therefore not included, as are religious orders or communities governed on a hierarchical basis and informal social movements.

(c) The Constitution must provide for a formal structure giving members the right to periodically elect a governing body and officers. There must be a permanent headquarters and commitment to sustainable operations. Hence, ad hoc committees or the organizing committee of a single international meeting are excluded.

(d) If for a period of time the management is of the same nationality, the organization is not necessarily disqualified, but in this case there should be a rotation at designated intervals of headquarters and officers among the various member countries.

(e) Substantial contributions to the budget must come from at least three countries, thereby excluding the many 'international' unions and societies operating in North America on budgets derived almost wholly from the United States members. There must be no attempt to make profits to distribute to members. This does not exclude organizations which exist in order to help members themselves make more profits or better their economic situation (for example, trade unions or trade associations); but it does exclude international business enterprises, investment houses and cartels. The distinction between a trade association and a cartel is often unclear; in practice the external relations of the body are used as a guideline.

(f) Entities formally connected with another organization are not necessarily excluded, but there must be evidence that they lead an independent life and elect their own officers. Internal or subsidiary committees, appointed by and reporting to one of the structural units of a given organization, are excluded.

(g) Evidence of current activity must be available; organizations which appear to have been inactive for over four years are eventually treated as 'dissolved' or 'dormant'.

(h) No directives are made as to size or 'importance', whether in terms of number of members, degree of activity or financial strength. No organizations are excluded on political or ideological grounds, nor are fields of interest or activity taken into consideration. The geographical location of the headquarters and the terminology used in the organization's name (whether 'committee', 'council', etc.) have likewise been held to be irrelevant in the determination of eligibility.

3. The London School of Economics (LSE). The LSE has established the following criteria for an international NGO: They are autonomous organizations; that is, they are not instruments of government; non-profit, that is, not distributing revenue as income to owners; and they have to be formal, legal entities (Salamon and Anheier 1997). According to the LSE's Civil Society Yearbook 2004–05, there are close to 20,000 NGOs operating on an international scale (Anheier et al. 2004).

Interestingly, the trans-national level has laid the groundwork for quantifying these types of organizations, whereas on the national level the key driver for registration has been tax relevant criteria, something not applicable for every organization operating in this field. However, their criteria for acknowledgement are very much applicable to transnational, mature organizations, whereas the numerous national, grassroots organizations remain uncounted. It is not known how many non-governmental organizations exist at the country level: in India alone, for example, it is estimated that there are over 1.2m non-governmental organizations according to the Voluntary Action Network India, the apex body of Indian NGOs. Of these, roughly only 9 per cent have ten or more employees on their payrolls. They often lack the skills and the research tools needed to actively position their agenda in the public so as to raise funds and initiate a dialogue on change.

EXPENDITURE

The John Hopkins Comparative non-profit project has tried to quantify the economic contribution of the NGO sector to an economy. For that, they have gathered information from 35 developing and developed countries for the period between 1995 to 1998. The statistics, despite being dated, point to the overall importance of the NGO sector:

1. The sector sees 1.3 trillion dollars in expenditure, equivalent to 5.1 per cent of combined expenditure.
2. It can be considered the world's seventh largest economy.
3. The NGO sector employs 39.5 million full-time equivalent employees or 4.4 per cent of the economically active population. In fact, this represents 10 times the number of employees in the utilities and textiles industries and 5 times the food manufacturing industry in these countries,
4. 190 million people volunteer for the NGO sector, representing more than 20 per cent of the population in these countries or the equivalent of 221 volunteers per 1,000 of the adult population (Salomon et al. 2003).

Nevertheless, detailed data on financial spending for this sector is not available at all. However, we do have a number of data points which help estimate the size of the sector. According to the latest study of the Center on Philanthropy at Indiana University released in December 2007, six in ten US households routinely contribute to charity. It is estimated that US citizens spend $219 billion per annum on non-governmental associations, equating to 2.31 per cent of the gross domestic product (GDP). In Germany, spending is around $7.5 billion or 0.36 per cent of GDP (Kunz 2006: 13). Overall, we can assume that contributions made by individuals and organizations into this sector are comparatively high, with only a limited number reporting on their revenues and spending. However, it is a major trend driven mainly by international organizations to increase transparency in the sector. The objective is not only to have a better understanding, but also to prevent fraud and misuse of development money.

FROM SOCIAL ACTIVISM TO SOCIAL ENTREPRENEURSHIP—KEY TRENDS

Successful NGOs started at the grassroots level, and their tremendous power to make moral arguments was often rooted in the strong opinions of their charismatic founders (Heins 2002: 133f). By making shortcomings strategically visible to the public they challenged governments and companies across the globe. Almost all of them have professionalized quite successfully. Greenpeace is surely one of the most well-known examples: The origins of Greenpeace lie in the Peace movement and the Campaign for Nuclear Disarmament generally, and in the 'Don't Make a Wave' Committee, co-founded by Jim and Marie Bohlen and formed by an assortment of Canadian and expatriate American peace activists in Vancouver in 1970, particularly. Today, Greenpeace has 27 national and regional offices around the world, providing a presence in 41 countries. It runs campaigns and projects which fit into the 'issues' (as campaign areas are called within Greenpeace) listed below. Greenpeace addresses issues such as over-fishing or threats linked to harmful nuclear radiation and nuclear proliferation. Furthermore, it campaigns for alternative solutions such as marine reserves and renewable energy. The latest publicly available annual report shows an income of almost €205 million, 98 per cent of which comes from grants and donations. Greenpeace has increased its global presence and impact through a new form of campaigning especially targeted at involving the media. The precedent for this event-driven media campaigning was the intervention against the disposal of the Brent Spar in the Atlantic in 1995. Brent Spar or Brent E, was an oil storage and tanker loading buoy in the Brent oilfield and operated by Shell UK. Greenpeace organized a worldwide media campaign against this plan. Although the watchdog never called for a boycott of Shell service stations, thousands of people stopped buying their petrol at Shell, and Greenpeace activists occupied the Brent Spar for more than three weeks. In the face of public and political opposition in northern Europe (including some physical attacks and an arson attack on a service station in Germany), Shell abandoned its plans to dispose of Brent Spar at sea – whilst continuing to stand by its claim that this was the safest option, both from an environmental and an industrial health and safety perspective. Following that event numerous papers looked at the specific role of media (Baringhorst 1998). Clearly, Brent Spar was the initial case of political communication because of the spectacular events brought to public attention worldwide. Greenpeace continues to successfully apply this form of political communication to create publicity for its agenda. Other NGOs like Robin Wood or Amnesty International have adopted similar communication strategies targeted at the public. Furthermore, Greenpeace stands for other trends in the NGO arena, which can overall be described as a trend for professionalization in public relations management. Other examples of successful social entrepreneurship are Oxfam's third-world-shops or the mail order trade of the World Wide Fund for Nature (WWF).

KEY CHALLENGES

In summary, access to funding, skills and support systems are the key challenges NGOs are facing today. The beneficial cause alone is not a guarantee for long term commitment of donors and volunteers, as competitions for funds and public attention is increasing. The major challenges NGOs are facing today can be described as follows:

1. Accessing sources of funding.
2. Defining the right organizational governance and operating model.
3. Raising the organization's profile with the government and the stakeholders.
4. Forming strategic partnerships with public and private sector entities.
5. Motivating employees and volunteers.

Successful organizations address those challenges through a set of management tools tailored to the needs of their sector.

1. Attention management.
2. Institutionalization of structured organizational governance.
3. Professional stakeholder management.
4. Invention of new business models to generate further revenues.
5. Increased financial transparency and accountability
6. Structured approach to integrate volunteers.

1. Attention Management

Competition for funds is increasing and one key differentiator for a successful NGO is to be associated with a cause which is at the centre of public attention. Furthermore, a successful NGO has to ensure that it is not forgotten. Presence in the media as well as at prominent events ensures a presence in the mind of the stakeholders. Here, a professional approach towards working with the media is a key success factor. The complexity of this requirement, however, increases with the geographic scope of an organization.

2. Institutionalization of Structured Organizational Governance

One key element of the increasing maturity of the NGOs sector is the emergence of the need for an organizational structure, including a clear division of labour and the definition of processes to deliver services or messages to the public. The internal structure, looking at human resources, finance, procurement, marketing or public relations, is often complemented by external advisory boards which act as an additional channel of access into wider groups in society. Typically, NGOs seek to engage people with a strong public image – celebrities or politicians – to raise their own profile to become a powerful brand.

3. Professional Stakeholder Management

Financially, NGOs depend largely on donations from national or international government bodies as well as people who have to have a somewhat altruistic drive to support them. Even more importantly, their public image, their brand as a knight in a shining armour for the good cause is very much influenced by what people say about them. Their stakeholders could potentially be any individual or organization affected by their actions; this includes supporters, employees and the wider community. In order to optimize donations as well as enlarge their public image, some NGOs started to segment their donors and supporters in order to give personalized messages. They also tailored marketing to address their needs – and coffers – more effectively.

4. Invention of New Business Models to Generate further Donations and/or Revenues

Donations are typically very volatile sources of income. When public attention is directed to a specific event, for example the tsunami in December 2004, donations are typically reduced for other organizations. Some NGOs have been quite successful in mitigating this risk through professional stakeholder management, but have also come up with strategies to increase revenues with alternate business models. Examples include events or branded goods such as t-shirts, posters or postcards. Overall, however, NGOs have not been successful in gathering significant revenues from these sources.

5. Increased Financial Transparency and Accountability

Various stakeholder groups of NGOs expect their organization to be able to verify the purpose for which they have utilized their financial and human resources. Not only the donors, but also trans-national governmental organizations like the UN and the EU are increasingly demanding comparable transparency standards for NPOs similar to what they request from profit organizations. Whereas a comparatively large number of trans-national organizations already publish annual reports containing a proper profit and loss statement as well as a listing of objectives, activities and achievements, smaller national organizations still do not do it, either because of a lack of perceived need or skills.

6. Structured Approach to Integrate Volunteers

NGOs have to rely to a large extent on volunteers 'to get the job done'. Smart organizations have learnt that they can significantly increase the amount of helping hands as help as well their skill base. A good example here would be Give India, an online portal matching providers and seekers of donation. Give India serves as a clearing house, ensuring that the NGO a donor is giving his money to can be considered trustworthy. Give India asks a small fee for their services which does not cover their operating costs. They rely on a network of supporters giving their skills for free. Often volunteers are very motivated but other than employees that are on the payroll, volunteers can more easily walk away if they are not motivated to continue their support. Some NGOs have started to institutionalize volunteer loyalty schemes, including the founding of local chapters or clubs, direct mailings or events. Furthermore, training provided through the organization enriches the volunteers' experience and helps to develop better results.

Chapter Two

India in Focus

WITH A population of 1.1 billion, India is the world's largest democracy, a nuclear power with an important seat at international institutions and increasingly a significant driver of the global economy. Even the most conservative forecasts place India among the world's top five economies by 2010 in terms of purchasing power parity (PPP). Based on the fundamental precepts set by Mahatma Gandhi, Indian civil society has a long tradition and is consequently very well positioned to drive the global development agenda. For example, Indian NGOs initiated the global march against child labour in 1998 and hosted the World Social Forum in 2004.

India is the gateway to Asia with a rising influence on policy formulation in both the Asia Pacific region as well as globally. Therefore, looking at ways to professionalize in the non-profit sector from an Indian perspective will add value to the overall dialogue on the changing role of the non-governmental sector in global governance. The emerging importance of India in economic, political and cultural terms legitimizes a fresh look at the NGO sector of the country. Going forward, it will surely be used as a benchmark for assessing key success factors for non-profits in Asia and the globe. In order to achieve that, we will profile selected Indian players with selected organizations from other parts of the world using an interview based, qualitative approach.

Indian NGOs are playing a central role in bringing the theme of inclusive growth to the fore. From an economic and social perspective inclusiveness is a prerequisite to sustainable growth given the ability to spread the benefits of this growth more widely. Beyond efficient and effective public services, the World Bank's last policy review on India stresses the importance of providing access to opportunities for a growing part of the population:

> Maintaining rapid growth will require more, and more effective, investments in infrastructure to create more jobs for low and semi-skilled workers. Growth should more equally be shared by all, as many parts of the country remain poor. Promoting inclusive growth includes revamping labour regulations, improving agricultural technology and infrastructure, helping lagging states and regions catch up, and empowering the poor through proactive policies that help them to take part in the market on fair and equitable terms. (World Bank 2006)

The role of Indian NGOs to ensure inclusive growth and social modernization in India can provide best practice examples for NGOs in other emerging markets across the globe.

GIVING IN INDIA

Giving in India is inseparable from religion and places of worship. Very often, it is guided by religion and the requirements of caste, family and community. Therefore, giving is deeply embedded in the Indian culture and is practiced in various types and forms by all members of the society, independent of income and status.

However, within the affluent groups in the country, often the practice of individual giving can be perceived as a central part of upper-class culture and identity (Ostrower 1995). Though there is only limited and quite dated data available, it gives an indication about the strength of this sector in India. A survey conducted in 2001 by Sampradaan, the Indian Centre for Philanthropy covering around 28 per cent of urban India concluded that 96 per cent of upper- and middle-class households in urban India donate to a charitable cause. This amount is reported to be around Rs 16 billion (US $34 million) annually. Another study on individual giving in five southern cities (Asian Philanthropy Consortium 2003) has also recorded a high incidence of giving, both in terms of size and frequency, among particular income groups. The study shows that a sample of 200 individuals donated an amount of Rs 0.5 million (US \$11,000) in one year. It also indicates that in the urban high-salaried class, giving has become more rationalized and people are willing to contribute to large foundations that can channel funds more effectively, rather than to governmental and religious institutions.

Corporate philanthropy in India has a very long history going back to the early 19th century. The corporate community of India is made up of different traditions arising particularly from religious and traditional backgrounds. In the Indian corporate scenario, different business communities like the Parsis, the Marwaris, the Khatris, the Reddys and the Chettiars were at the forefront of philanthropic activities. Institutionalized philanthropy also received an impetus with the industrial revolution in India, as corporate wealth began to be channelled towards welfare and development work. Indian companies have done a fantastic job in building generous philanthropy programs, something that multinationals can certainly learn from. For example, the Tata Trust can hardly be rivalled anywhere in the world. This philanthropy is very often tied to the personal history of the giver and his family. However, the broader concept of 'corporate citizenship' has evolved tremendously over recent years among multinational companies (MNCs). Corporate citizenship for many MNCs is now closely linked to the overall strategy of the firm and involves all company stakeholders, including employees, customers, associations as well as the wider society.

It is also evident that some NGOs are taking proactive steps to develop higher value-added skills and capabilities; and for India, much of this will contribute to the domestic ecosystem and ALL of it will benefit the country. Important areas that need to be worked on to ensure inclusive growth in India include:

1. Education — particularly in developing more independent and lateral thinking.
2. Health — providing equal access, particularly in the countryside.

3. Equality and access — ensuring life opportunities for many, regardless of social background and gender.
4. Innovation — A broader 'innovation ecosystem' where government, private sector and academia are much better networked to build synergies and efficient mechanisms to capitalize on the creation of new ideas, products and services.

SNAPSHOT OF THE INDIAN NGO SECTOR

As data on the Indian non-profit sector are limited, we have to work with rough estimates, often lumping together a whole variety of groups and organizations under the umbrella of non-profits. This, however, is true for the whole globe, where NGOs — despite being a key driver for civil society — are not well understood. According to Participatory Research in Asia (PRIA), the International Centre for Learning and Promotion of Participation and Democratic Governance in India, there are roughly 1.2 million NGOs in India, largely based and operating in rural areas (PRIA 2002). Many of them are not incorporated legally: the percentage of non-registered organizations is lowest in Tamil Nadu (47 per cent) and highest in Maharastra (74 per cent). There are, however, a number of NGOs which can be considered illegal, pursuing other than good causes, but they are not within the scope of this book.

Overall, Indian NGOs are essentially very small in size: only 8.5 per cent of the organizations employ more than 10 per cent of paid staff. Almost two-thirds have one or no paid staff, relying to a large extent on volunteers. However, nearly 20 million people work on a paid or voluntary basis in non-profit organizations. This number shows the importance of NGOs both as employers and as agencies providing identity and belonging to communities.

Their major activities are:

1. Religious (engaged in social development through primary identity as a religious institution) (26.5 per cent)
2. Community/social services (21.3 per cent)

3. Education (20.4 per cent)
4. Sports/culture (18 per cent)
5. Health (6.6 per cent)

According to this source, NGOs overall receive an estimated $4 million per annum. Interestingly, only 7.4 per cent of total donations originate from foreign funds.

According to the Asian Philanthropic Society the last few years have seen significant shifts in the regulation of the non-profit sector and philanthropy in India. This is partly because of the high profile that NGOs now enjoy in India, and partly as an attempt to overhaul the Indian legal and fiscal regulations relating to NPOs — shifts that in some cases lead toward greater control over the non-profit sector and its activities, and in other cases lead toward greater autonomy for the sector. There have been developments in a number of areas and these are highlighted below:

1. Renewed proposals and debates on amendment to the Foreign Contributions (Regulation) Act 1976, which governs foreign donations to the Indian non-profit sector;
2. Changes in the fiscal policy, particularly taxation, where many exemptions are under review and some have already been modified, as well as changes in the Stamp Act, Value Added Tax Act 2005 and other fiscal legislation;
3. Pressures for newer money laundering legislation and related regulations on anonymous donations;
4. New proposals to regulate the micro-finance sector;
5. Implications of the Right to Information Act 2005 for the Indian voluntary sector.

(Asian Philanthropy Consortium 2007)

Perhaps the most important and far-reaching change has been the approval and announcement of a national policy on the voluntary sector. This policy, drafted and finalized after consultations with the non-profit sector and various government departments, is intended to provide a framework for partnership between the government and the voluntary sector. More specifically, the policy is intended to create an enabling environment for the voluntary sector, to enhance their resource mobilization capacity and to encourage accountability and transparency in the sector.

It must be noted that this new national policy on the voluntary sector is not a binding law, only a statement of intention. It does not bind the government to a specific time-frame or commit it to pass new laws or amend old ones. Much will depend on these aspects of implementation, both at the central level and in the states. But the national policy on the voluntary sector is a significant step forward (Asian Philanthropy Consortium 2007).

Chapter Three

The Role of Political
Communication in Agenda Setting

WHY IS political communication important? The history of political organizations, be it political parties, political interest groups or NGOs is also a history of political communication. Depending on the technological possibilities, political organizations have communicated with citizens in various ways during different stages of their development (Farrell and Webb 2000; Römmele and Gibson 2001). The earliest forms of campaigning were characterized by face-to-face communication among party members and voters, and mass event rallies organized by political organizations were dominant. During the second or 'modern' era of political communication, there was a switch to the more impersonal channel—that is, the mass media, especially TV. In the past decade, a third mode of campaigning has emerged in post-industrial democracies. While initially this was referred to, in generic terms, as the Americanized style of campaigning (Negrine and Papathanassopoulos 1996), recently it has had more historical or developmental labels applied to it, such as post-modern (Norris 2000), phase 3 (Farrell and Webb 2000) and post-Fordism (Nadesan 2001). Despite these differences in nomenclature, there is considerable agreement among these scholars as to the central features of this new era of political communication. The most widely used tools of professionalized political communication are the following:

1. Telemarketing

   (a) contacting own members.
   (b) contacting outside target groups.

2. Direct mail

   (a) to own members.
   (b) to outside target groups.

3. Presence of an internal internet communication system.
4. Email 'sign-up' or subscription list for regular news updates.
5. Locations outside campaign headquarters.
6. Continuous campaigning.
7. Use of external public relations/media consultants.
8. Use of computerized databases.
9. Use of opinion polling.
10. The conducting of opposition research.

The relationship between political entities and the media can best be described as symbiotic—they cannot live without one another. The media on the one hand needs information from the political actors and these on the other hand need publicity for their political agenda.

In general, political organizations compete for the limited attention of citizens. In the era of modern campaigning, political parties (in particular the larger organizations), particularly compared to NGOs, clearly have had better chances to attract attention since their connection to the media system was either better or closer. However, in the era of professionalized campaigning this has changed.

Looking at the development of political communication and especially at the tools at hand in the era of professionalized political communication, it provides less formalized political organizations such as protest networks, flash campaigns or NGOs, a tremendous opportunity. Because of the relatively low cost of the internet and the lack of an editorial control fringe, campaigns have greater opportunities to voice their concerns and get their message across than they did via the traditional media. Moreover, email and hypertext links make it easier than before to mobilize protest quickly and link together previously unconnected individuals, even breaking down traditional barriers between space and time. One recent example from the US primaries and the race between Hillary Clinton and Barack Obama showed how smart usage of online political campaigning and fundraising can make a real difference. In 2006 Hillary Clinton was able to raise $51.6 million through big cheque writers. Since then, the law has changed and donations above $2300 are not being allowed. The Clintons had to tap into their own fortune to pay for the Super Tuesday ($5 million) and then another time ($6.4 million) to get her through the Indiana and North Carolina primaries. Obama relied on another model: more than 800,000 people had signed up on his website and continued to contribute in the $5, $10 or $50 range. Obama raised more than $100 million online from his supporters regardless of their income (Weisskopf 2008). Technological innovations have enabled NGOs to influence the ideas, values, political convictions and perceptual models of people all over the world (Take 2000: 202). The potency of email and the internet as mobilizing tools have been seen in a number of recent mass demonstrations and rallies, not least of all the anti-globalization protests in Seattle in 1999 and the Stop the War rallies in 2003. Arguably, it is these decentralized, formalized types of networks that offer greater flexibility to experiment with the technology and exploit its interactive potential, since they are not held back by formal organizational rules or hierarchical chains of command. Thus, some of the more novel uses of technology such as political hacking, virtual sit-ins and blockades have come from informal protest networks, particularly in environmental and human rights and social justice fields. As never before, tiny but creative and flexible organizations can raise awareness and mobilize protest on a large geographical scale. However, to agree upon actions and to institutionalize change, other skills and capabilities are needed.

In summary, political communication can be considered as the main means to position one's agenda in the public for pursuing organizational objectives. The process of being visible in public is a prerequisite for success. Prior to that, though, a thoughtful assessment of one's strategic positioning is necessary.

CONCEPT OF THE PUBLIC

Contemporary thinking on the public sphere is predominantly based on Jürgen Habermas' book *The Structural Transformation of the Public Sphere – An Inquiry into a Category of Bourgeois Society*.[1] The term 'public sphere' refers to an inclusive spatial concept, social sites like the web or public arenas where opinions are articulated, distributed and negotiated, regardless of people's background, status or professional role. The concept goes back to the 18th century, with liberal democracy having its seed in the bourgeois public sphere. It was separated from the power of both the church and the government due to its access to a variety of resources, both economic and social. Overall, the underlying concept is that public reasoning provides the basis for shared and therefore democratic decisions on governance of community, society and the state. However, this peculiar function of the public sphere has been weakened since then. The state has started to interfere and more importantly, proactive usage of the communicative power of the public sphere such as interest groups to pursue private interests rather than public good has changed the character of the democratic space. Today, the public sphere is actively used in an interactive process involving political communicators, media professionals and citizens to set agendas, influence public decision making or initiate policy change. From an arena of deliberate exchange of ideas, the public sphere has transformed itself into a managed entity where political interests are represented through political communication. An understanding of the dynamics of the public – the communicative tools used to be visible and heard – are a prerequisite for political success. Many NGOs, social movements, interest groups, political parties and sometimes individuals have effectively used the power of public presence to achieve their objectives.

IS ASIA DIFFERENT?

The historical point of emergence, size and policy focus of the non-profit sector in a country is an outcome of the specific relationship between state, market and civil society of which NGOs are a key part. However, regardless of place or time, civil society typically emerges as a function of increasing democratization and drive for reform. In India, which has a rich history in civil society, the first institution to foster social reform by looking after elderly people was established by Rev. Loveless in Madras as early as 1807 (Sooryamoorthy and Gangrade 2006). Activities by Indian philanthropists and missionaries combined, established a network of various institutions across the country. These brought into focus social reform and welfare-related questions, and the emerging freedom movement added to the wealth of organizations in India. Independence fuelled civil society and proved the correlation between democracy and civil society.

This twin phenomenon of civil society and increasing democratization has captured the imagination of intellectuals, activists, political leaders and policy-makers and therefore continues to catalyze the international community to strengthen NGOs to foster democracy and inclusion. Whereas the size and variety of the NGO sector normally can be taken as an indicator for further democratization; agents, policy fields and the way they work with governments, tend to differ in Asia, Europe and the US.

Other than the US and Europe, where national NGOs are often community-based interest groups, NGOs in Asia have been emerging with increasing democratization and inclusion, covering for the shortcomings of the welfare state. This process has often been facilitated and sponsored by international NGOs. They tend to focus on issues in their own country, whereas in mature economies many NGOs work in the area of trans-national collaboration and development. Duke University in the US has compiled an impressive online database of NGOs by region, showing the variety in policy field and outreach.[2] China is a good example of an emerging civil society, in which NGOs step-in to fulfil citizens' needs in a number of policy fields, where the state has been unable to do so.

In China, there are about 2 million NGOs which have come into existence in the past two decades. They are an important force for closing the gaps in the Chinese welfare state, especially for the current Chinese social, health and ecological policies. In China, NGOs operate under challenging conditions because of the ambivalent approach taken by the government.

> On the one hand, NGO work is supported because there is a need to compensate for the social, economic, and ecological consequences which have accompanied the politics of reform since 1978. On the other hand, the government poses high political and legislative restrictions on NGOs, so that an overwhelming number of them cannot be officially registered and, therefore, are forced to work in an illegal or semi-legal context. Many organizations register de jure as NGOs, but are de facto outsourced administrative bodies. (Brie and Pietzker 2004)

ROLE OF THE MEDIA IN ASIA

Historically, the media as the 'fourth power' has played a central role during the emergence of civil society and democracy. In India, the free press played a crucial role in the era of strife for independence. *The Hindu*, published by the Kasturi family from Chennai since 1878, was the first independent Indian newspaper and has been one of the key ambassadors of a free and independent India. Communication through the media plays a crucial role all over Asia, as it does across the globe. Many NGOs successfully use the media as a channel to raise awareness for their major objectives.

Because of political, economic and social circumstances, different types of media systems have come into existence (Hallin and Mancini 2004).

Basically, national media can be described and compared through three indicators:

1. Is there a free press?
2. Is there an open or a monopolistic media market?
3. Is the media publicly or privately owned?

Freedom of the Press

Freedom House, a US based non-profit organization, surveys and assesses the state of the freedom of the press on a global scale. According to its 2007 survey, the number of countries judged as *free* stood at 90, representing 47 per cent of the world's 193 polities and 3,028,190,000 people — 46 per cent of the global population. The number of countries qualifying as *partly free* stood at 60, or 31 per cent of all countries assessed by the survey, and they comprised 1,185,300,000 people, or 18 per cent of the world's total. Forty-three countries were judged *not free*, that is, 22 per cent of the total polities. The number of people living under *not free* conditions stood at 2,391,400,000, or 36 per cent of the world population, although it is important to note that about half of this number lives in just one country — China. India, despite being by far the freest in South Asia, is only considered to be partly free. Of the 40 countries in the Asia Pacific region, 40 per cent (16) are considered to have a free press, including countries like New Zealand, Australia, Hong Kong, and others. One quarter (10 countries) are judged to be partly free, which are, not including India, Thailand, the Philippines and Cambodia. According to Freedom House, 35 per cent (14 countries), including Vietnam, Singapore, North Korea and China do not have a free press.

Open or Monopolistic Media Market?

Asia has three main forms of political governance impacting the structure of the market: an authoritarian, one-party system such as in China, Vietnam, North Korea or Laos; constitutional monarchies like Japan, Thailand or Cambodia and liberal parliamentary democracies like India or South-Korea. China as an example of an authoritarian one-party system has a monopolistic media market. Despite the fact that the Chinese constitution from 1982 has guaranteed free expression of opinion and freedom of press, the state of public freedom can only be described as precarious. Media and TV channels are owned and run by the government.

Interestingly, in the 1980s, a number of yellow press publications emerged and they continue to be in conflict with state authorities (Thomaß 2007: 300*ff*.). Despite ongoing international protests, China still maintains control of the internet and bans content from free broadcasting stations like the German *Deutsche Welle* and others. The main communication channel for the state continues to be the cinema, of which China has over 120,000 (US has 40,000).

Japan as an example for a constitutional monarchy has put a lot of emphasis on the printed press and can be considered an open market. The Japanese newspapers *Yomiuri* and *Asahi* together have a daily run of 27 million which makes them one of the highest print media circulations in the world. As in other constitutional monarchies, the large newspapers tend to be in favour of the ruling power. However, they also tend to play the role of the king's jester, addressing shortcomings in a specific way. India as an example of a parliamentary democracy has an open market for press and media. There are over 4000 dailies published in 20 languages across the country, numerous TV channels and a movie industry which has been spreading its profitable wings into other parts of the world.

Is the Media Publicly or Privately Owned?

Correspondingly, media in constitutional monarchies (for example Japan) or in parliamentary democracies (for example India) are more likely to be privately owned, whereas in an authoritarian one-party system the media is owned by the state.

NOTES

1. *The Structural Transformation of the Public Sphere: An Inquiry into a Category of Bourgeois Society* (in German: *Strukturwandel der Öffentlichkeit. Untersuchungen zu einer Kategorie der bürgerlichen Gesellschaft*), by Jürgen Habermas, was published in 1962 and translated into English in 1989 by Thomas Burger and Frederick Lawrence.
2. Duke University Library. 'NGO Research Guide'. Available online at http://library.duke.edu/research/subject/guides/ngo_guide (Accessed on 8 August 2007).

Chapter Four

Some Best Practice Case Studies

WHY USE CASE STUDIES?

W E CONDUCTED interviews with six NGOs in India in the policy fields of health, children's rights, HIV and environment; and furthermore one European, one American as well as one trans-national NGO. We have chosen this approach for two reasons.

First, the collection of case studies is a powerful academic approach for providing a detailed contextual analysis. Other than quantitative, statistical methodologies—and we will come to this later—the qualitative approach of presenting case studies is not targeted as presenting a universal truth. The emphasis here is placed on description and exploration (Lijphart 1971). Researcher Robert K. Yin defines the case study research method as an empirical inquiry that investigates a contemporary phenomenon within its real-life context; when the boundaries between phenomenon and context are not clearly evident and in which multiple sources of evidence are used (Yin 1984: 23).

Second, field work enables us to illustrate the strategic tools which are being introduced in this book. We feel that showcasing real life examples of successful usage of the tools contributing to the success of an organization's goals shows their relevance in a more compelling way. They might serve as 'food for thought' for NGOs, associations or interest groups so that they may explore the applicability of certain strategic processes presented here for their own undertakings. Although the organizations presented here differ significantly regarding organizational size and structure and policy field, all the NGOs considered have been very successful regarding specific aspects of their communication strategies. This approach allows one to gain insights into the communication efforts of different organizations with different approaches and different regulatory frameworks. As we introduce our strategic toolbox to initiate policy change, we draw upon a hypothetical case study of an NGO working to address the question of HIV/AIDS.

BEST PRACTICE CASE STUDIES

We have selected case study examples (see Table 4.1) from a random sample based on their best practice in some of the areas discussed in this book. The focus is on India and the role of NGOs in modernizing and advancing the country, ensuring inclusive growth and equality.

TABLE 4.1
Best Practice Case Studies

Name	Founding Year	Area
Amnesty International Germany	1961 in London	Berlin/Germany
The Banyan	1993	Chennai/India
Butterflies	1989	New Delhi/India
iCONGO	2004	New Dehli/India
Indian Network for people living with AIDS/HIV (INP+)	1997	Chennai/India
MV Foundation	1981	Secunderabad/India
Room to Read	1998	San Francisco/US
Young European Federalists (JEF)	1949	Brussels/Belgium

Source: Compiled by the authors.

Amnesty International operates on a global level and has set benchmarks in the way human rights violations are addressed. They are a member-based organization and have a very structured and compelling way of conducting public relations and campaigning. They are considered the trusted adviser globally when it come to securing universal human rights—their professionalism and neutrality makes them respected all across the globe.

The Banyan is a Chennai-based, Indian NGO looking after mentally ill, homeless women. The Banyan pursues its objectives through an employee-based organization and has access to a large and influential group of donors and supporters all across India. Apart from their contribution through social work and advocacy, they are now seeking to improve education and leadership among mental illness practitioners through their academic arm, the Banyan Institute for Leadership in Mental Illness. This holistic approach to their area of focus as well as to stakeholder management can be considered a best practice.

Butterflies is based in New Delhi, India and operates country-wide in the area of children's rights. It provides its services through its employees and maintains a large partner network through which it can provide a large portfolio of services to street children. It uses a unique and compelling approach for integrating the street kids through open discussions and forums where kids give voice to their specific needs. One impressive idea raised in one of these forums, and now manifested, was to institutionalize a children's development bank to educate street kids in financial management.

iCONGO, Confederation of NGOs is a Delhi-based organization, giving voice and expertise to their 70 members. Its differentiator is to equip its members with state-of-the-art political communication tools. It uses sophisticated communication strategies to deliver its message and concerns through the media. For that, it uses the iCONGO Media Service (IMS) to help their partner NGOs in positioning their press releases and related information with media houses. They have also launched a 24/7 media news portal www.dishoooom.com at which everybody can write in and share their views on any social- or cause-related issues.

INP+ is a network of, for and by people living with HIV/AIDS in India. The NGO is headquartered in Chennai and has over 100,000 members across the country. Apart from social and medical services, the organization uses a unique approach: to decrease stigmatization and increase prevention — INP+ trains their members to act as 'positive speakers'. Its approach to integrating patients into educating the population raises its overall presence and more importantly, is an important source of self-respect for infected people.

MV Foundation in Secundarabad, is an India-based organization that works in the policy field of children's rights, promoting their entitlement to education and for this reason campaigns against child labour. Today, it monitors and supports 400,000 children in India. The MV Foundation is a member-based organization which operates across the country. A unique feature is that it works within the local 'ecosystem' in the communities so as to convince key decision makers and, through them, the people, to pursue education for their kids.

Room to Read is an NGO with headquarters in the US. The organization was founded by a former Microsoft executive with the objective to increase literacy and correspondingly to provide access to opportunities in life. The NGO can be considered a best practice in applying principles from business whilst still maintaining the spirit of a non–profit organization with the goal to make the world a better place.

Young European Federalist (JEF) is Brussels based organization that promotes the vision of a united, federal and democratic Europe. JEF is a volunteer-based organization and has supporters in more than 30 countries. Its unique feature is that it promotes a political concept to make it attractive and understandable. It stands out through its international, mainly virtual, organization which operates exactly on the principle it promotes: federalism.

Chapter Five

A Framework for Initiating Policy Change

There are no secrets to success. It is the result of preparation,
hard work, and learning from failure.

Colin Powell

INITIATING POLICY change is a process involving an understanding of the political context as well as the underlying assumptions of policy formulation by key decision makers (Hovland and Start 2004).

It involves:

1. identifying the issue and finding evidence for it;
2. developing one's position;
3. communicating one's objectives considering the specific political ecosystem in which the issue resides; and
4. lobbying and advocacy as additional drivers for decision makers to consider change.

The main objective is to use insight, and communicate it for political impact. It assumes the capacity to generate, acquire, assimilate and utilize knowledge to form a crucial part of the strategies to achieve objectives. This, enabled and enriched through aggressive marketing techniques, will help bring a specific issue to the fore, ideally resulting in support from the public and key stakeholders and increasing pressure on policy-makers to react.

FIGURE 5.1
A Framework for Initiating Policy Change

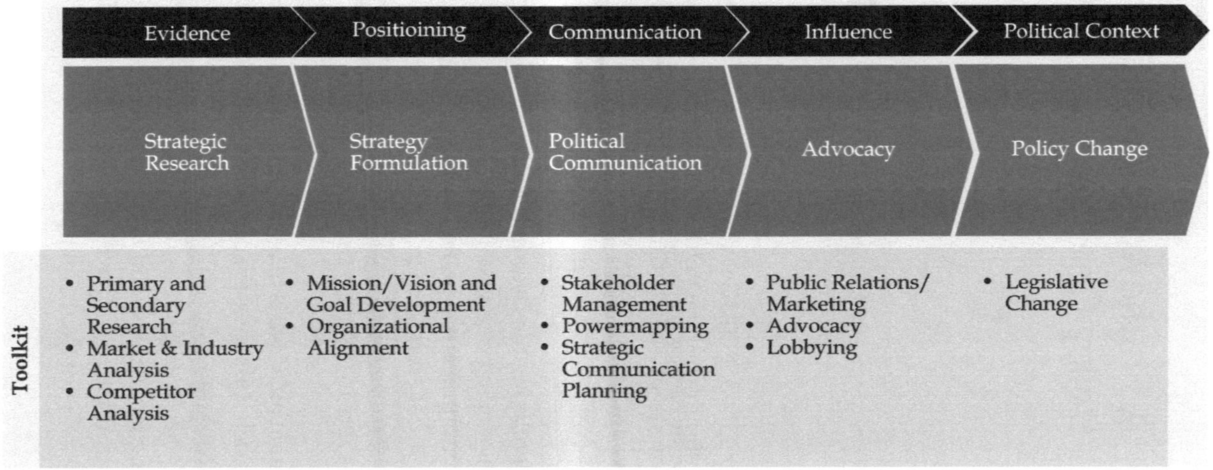

Evidence	Positioining	Communication	Influence	Political Context
Strategic Research	Strategy Formulation	Political Communication	Advocacy	Policy Change
• Primary and Secondary Research • Market & Industry Analysis • Competitor Analysis	• Mission/Vision and Goal Development • Organizational Alignment	• Stakeholder Management • Powermapping • Strategic Communication Planning	• Public Relations/ Marketing • Advocacy • Lobbying	• Legislative Change

Toolkit

Source: Developed by the authors.

Academics, practitioners in strategy consulting or market research, as well as international organizations and social activists have created a number of tools we can use in order to support initiatives for policy change. We will discuss many, but not all, of them on the following pages. We have tried to choose the ones most relevant for this purpose — one may pick and choose what is the most helpful in a specific situation. Trying to go for the 'full suit' implies the opportunity to review your underlying assumptions at any point of your thought process. Figure 5.1 is a blueprint for initiating policy change and a selection of strategic tools to be used during the process. We will walk along the same road using a case study which we came up with for the purpose of making it less theoretical. Apart from our illustration, we will integrate the best practice examples from our interviews.

> Imagine the following: you are a teacher in a kindergarten in a disadvantaged community in a large Indian city. It is brought to your attention that in the last couple of months the number of school kids infected with HIV/AIDS has increased. You are shocked: what should be done with those kids? Exclude them from class to protect the other kids? Speak to the community head to find an alternate solution for them? Work with the city council ...the state or national Ministry of Health ...or better yet the Ministry of Youth? You don't know what to do, but it really feels that it is necessary to act upon this situation. To start with, you look around the country and you discover that this problem is not isolated to your community. It is a country-wide phenomenon. You make up your mind: you have to do something significant about is and thus you found your NGO the same day! You decide to call it Prevent Our Children from AIDS (POCA). Luckily, the head of your kindergarten, a number of parents and the community head are as engaged as you are and have promised time and some financial support to help you get going! In the beginning you apply our framework for initiating policy change to make yourself heard, gain sponsorship, increase support and get funding to launch your NGO, first in your home city and then later nationwide.

The following pages will introduce a toolbox to strategically address those points.

MANAGING THE PROJECT

> *Plans are nothing. Planning is everything.*
>
> Dwight D. Eisenhower

Over the next couple of pages we will introduce the strategy toolbox to address the key question on how to best set up your NGO. It is not required to follow each of the steps outlined here to come up with a thorough strategy; your key questions might make some of them irrelevant. However, in all cases a project plan has to be in place. The main objective of all the undertakings is to reduce complexity in setting up an NGO, and to successfully find support and position it in your country. Therefore, a project plan developed in discussions with key stakeholders is the best start. It should contain milestones to get their agreement and buy-in.

A high-level work-plan, hypothetically, could look like Figure 5.2:

The work plan should not only contain tasks, number of resources, timing (1 man-day [MD] is typically eight hours) but a number of points ensuring that everybody is on the same page regarding the overall objective of that effort:

1. Purpose, objective and scope—this answers the question why we are undertaking this effort, what we want to achieve, which issues we want to focus on and what is it that has been defined as being 'within scope' of this exercise.
2. Overview of key questions and proposed methodology— here key questions and the tools to address the same are listed. The toolbox listed below will provide a set of options to use.
3. Governance of the project—here the team running the project gets introduced. Typically, it should include a project manager, a project team and a steering committee, including your key stakeholders as well as a quality team, which ideally should be from the outside so as to ensure neutrality (see Figure 5.3). This defines accountability for different parts of the undertaking. As a new NGO, it could be used to build relationships and create ownership with people considered key stakeholders.

FIGURE 5.2
Overview of High Level Work Plan

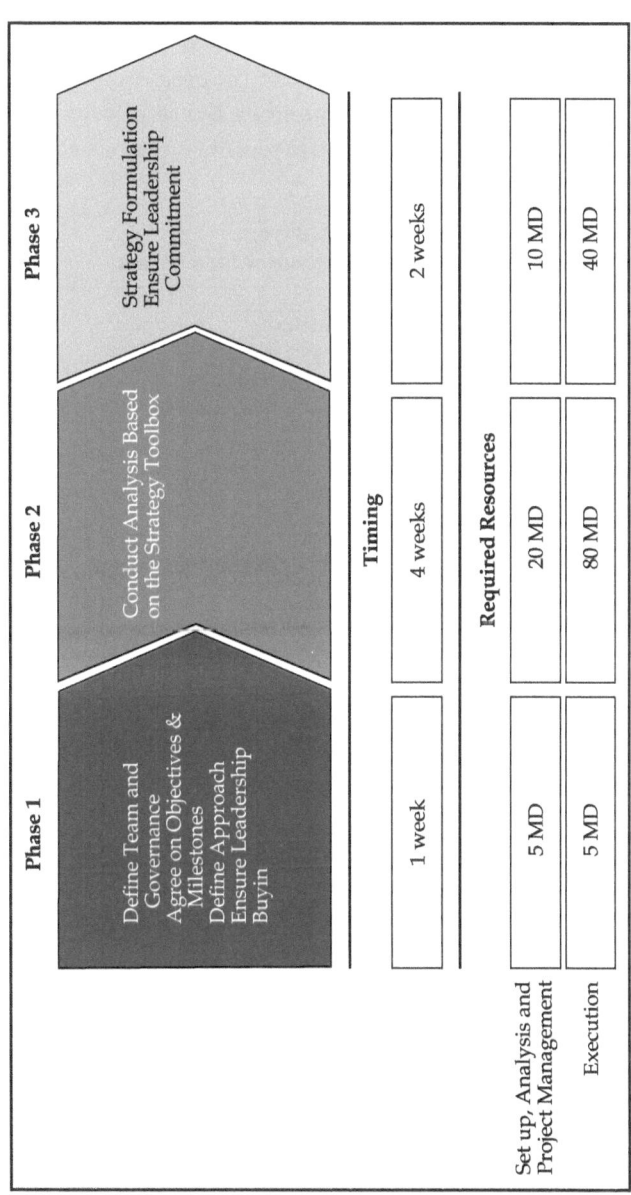

Source: Developed by the authors.

4. Timing — you assign deadlines to certain tasks and define the people who are responsible for it as per your governance. An important part of the timing is to define milestones which enable you not only to properly track progress and achievements and communicate the results and liaise with key stakeholders, but also to revisit your approach and make changes if needed.

FIGURE 5.3
Example of Governance for a Project

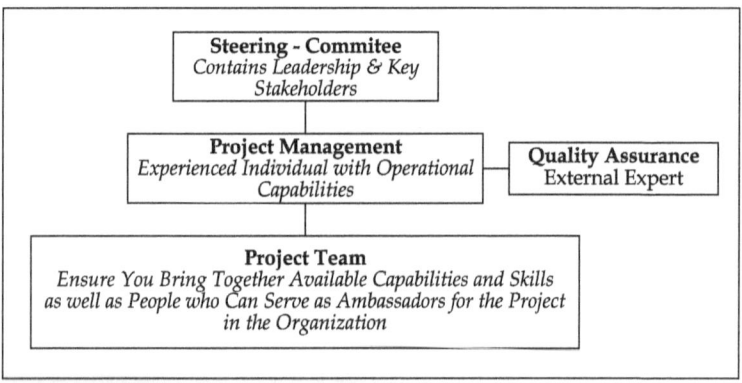

Source: Developed by the authors.

FORMULATING THE KEY QUESTION

In order to get started, it is important to be crystal clear about what has to be achieved. So it is paramount to come up with a key question in the beginning. The following section will help you to get there in a structured manner.

> Questions to be answered by POCA are:
> - How do I define my key question to start with?
> - How can I reduce my complex problem into workable chunks?
> - How do I define the hypothesis of what needs to be done in order to address the key problem, which in this case is reducing the number of kids with HIV/AIDS?

PROBLEM DEFINITION

For every complex problem there is a simple solution that is wrong.

George Bernard Shaw

Where to start? How to identify the right places and ways that are required to become a full-impact NGO? While it is important to talk to people intensively and to get them onboard to make the change, it is even more crucial to formulate a strategy early on. It will be fundamental to understand the different dimensions of the problem and the real needs of the community by looking at health and welfare services available to those already affected as well as determining the ways to prevent further expansion of the problem. It is crucial to identify potential donors and stakeholders by asking the following questions:

1. Who will make your organization stronger?
2. Who is operating in the same field and could be a potential partner for you so you can offer more services than you would be able to alone?
3. With whom are you competing for potential sponsors and public attention?

Many questions, the most important thing is to formulate the key questions so you can start formulating a strategy.

It is important not to underestimate this point. Often organizations come up with strategies to address non-existing problems and spend lots of money and resources.

> The key question to start formulating a strategy for POCA therefore would be: 'How can I reduce the number of children with HIV/AIDS in India?'

Without having answered this question properly, ideally in discussions with your key stakeholders, one shouldn't even start to strategize.

At this point, one might argue that the business concept of performance in the non-profit sector differs significantly from the domain of business. NGOs are not 'in business' to make profits. However, they are expected to use resources efficiently and to set goals for measuring their performance. Also, if they are not seen and heard they are not very likely to make an impact at all.

Developing a strategy is not an end in itself, but a means for reaching one's objectives. Your organization exists to fulfil a purpose and strategies are employed to ensure that the purpose is realized. Structuring one's thinking during the strategy process will help strengthen the approach and also help in determining a direction for making better decisions.

PROBLEM SOLVING

> *If the only tool you have is a hammer, you treat everything like a nail.*
>
> Abraham Maslow

Now the team is in place, leadership and key stakeholders have agreed on the strategy process (see Figure 5.4). Thus one can start with the most critical part of your effort, which as mentioned, is the key question addressed in this first and very important part of the strategy process:

What is the Problem I want to Solve?

Being the CEO of a young and immature NGO, your goal is to reduce the number of children infected with HIV/AIDS.

Through strategic problem-solving, you assess problems in a structured, hypothesis-driven manner. All major consulting firms apply some kind of tool-set to start their strategy process which is the key asset of a strategist. However you might call it—fact-based problem solving, a hypothesis-driven approach or applying the issue tree—you always go about business and organizational problems in a rigorously structured manner.

FIGURE 5.4
The Strategy Process

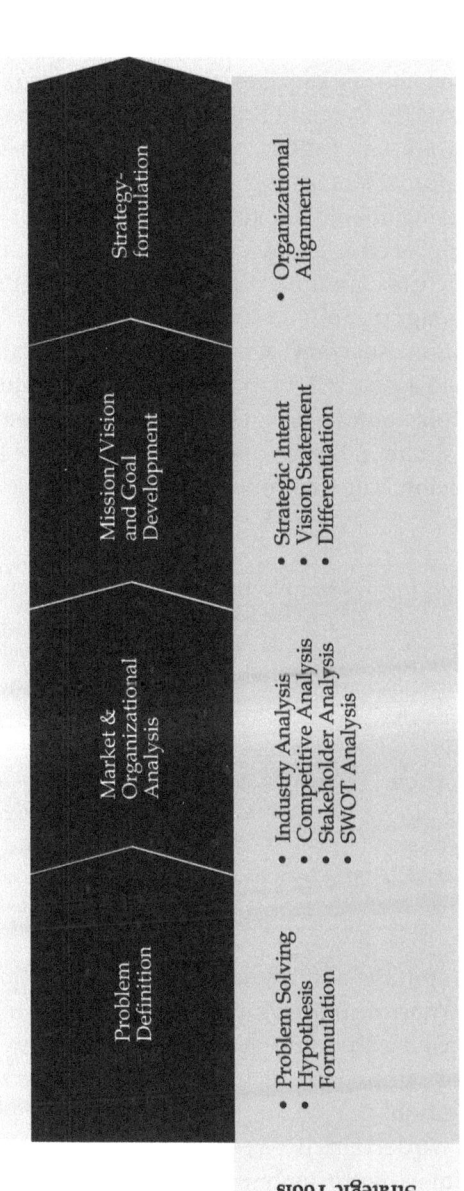

	Problem Definition	Market & Organizational Analysis	Mission/Vision and Goal Development	Strategy-formulation
Strategic Tools	• Problem Solving • Hypothesis Formulation	• Industry Analysis • Competitive Analysis • Stakeholder Analysis • SWOT Analysis	• Strategic Intent • Vision Statement • Differentiation	• Organizational Alignment

Source: Developed by the author.

Where to Start?

As mentioned, the first step is to identify the problem. Barbara Minto has introduced the Pyramid Principle to go about complex problems in a structured way (Minto 1996). Her Situation–Complication–Question approach helps to nail down the issue, the prerequisite to start thinking about your strategy. The situation–complication–question approach is a powerful structuring technique, mainly used to structure communication in all types and form. However, it also helps significantly to structure a problem.

S—Situation: Relevant facts about the organization's situation or the facts in a policy field; facts that nobody would dispute.

C—Complication: The trigger; the event, problem, and so on, in the client's situation that created the need for this communication.

Q—Question: The one fundamental issue this communication will address.

Applying this to our example, the structure would look as follows:

Situation: The number of children infected with HIV/AIDS has increased significantly. It is evident that the major parts of infections were transferred to the foetus by the mother. However, some of the infections resulted from insufficient preventions.
Complication: The needs of this specific group have not been addressed by specific policies or institutions, thereby resulting in social exclusion.
Question: What steps should POCA* take to decrease number of kids infected?

Common pitfalls of formulating a question is that they are too broad or too narrow or assumption driven. But in our example we have been asking the right question and can now continue. The next step for our analysis is to investigate the issues underlying our key question.

For that, we deconstruct a complex problem into smaller issues making them easier to analyse (see Figure 5.5).

One needs to ensure that all issues listed are mutually exclusive and collectively exhaustive (MECE), meaning that you don't list anything twice and include all relevant items.

FIGURE 5.5
The Issue Tree

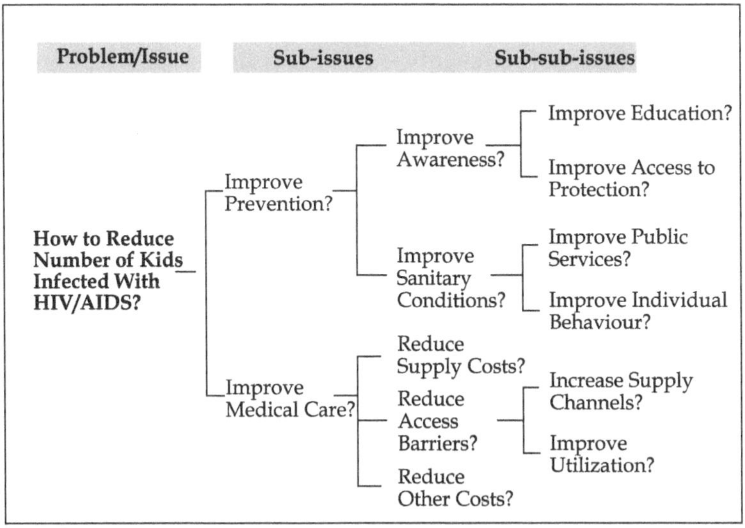

Source: Developed by the authors.

HYPOTHESIS FORMULATION

Where there is much desire to learn, there of necessity will be much arguing, much writing, many opinions; for opinion in good men is but knowledge in the making.

John Milton

Now, as the issue has been identified, one can start the necessary analysis. A worksheet (see Table 5.1) will help here.

TABLE 5.1
Issue Worksheet

Issue/Sub-Issue	Hypothesis	Data	Analysis
Lack of awareness of link between sexual behaviour, hygiene and infection	Increasing awareness will improve prevention	Collect data from UN AIDS or national groups which have assessed the correlation; collect data from the community and compare	Statistical analysis

Source: Developed by the authors.

We are now in the position to formulate our hypothesis about the problem we want to solve. In our case, we need to address the issue from a number of angles: working with communities and parents to improve prevention and providing a life with dignity for the kids affected.

This way, you can easily identify the points you need to address, thereby increasing donations and reducing costs in the organization at the same time.

You are now excited because you have kicked off an important part toward setting up your organization. However, to manage your expectations and to see the difference you are now starting to make will take a couple of months!

After the initial steps of the analysis, POCA has understood the following:

1. The main objective of the organization is to reduce the number of children in India with HIV/AIDS.
2. There is a need to improve awareness as well as access to medical treatment.

MV Foundation, one of our best practice case studies, works very closely with community leaders to increase awareness about the importance of education. It does this in a moderating, collaborative way, building on the existing power structure in the communities they work with. This top down approach ensures leadership buy-in and success of the programme.

Best Practice Example: MV Foundation

Vision/Mission

The work of the MV Foundation (MVF) is based on a firm conviction that no child should work and that all children between 5 and 14 must be at school enjoying freedom and dignity. According to the Foundation, there is an inextricable link between total abolition of child labour and universalization of school education. They are two sides of the same coin. Therefore the NGO addresses the issue of child labour as one of the main inhibitors of proper schooling and vice-versa.

Their Charter of Basic Principles for Emancipation of Child Labour spells out their principles, which they consider non-negotiable:

1. All children must attend full-time formal day schools.
2. Any child out of school is a child labourer.
3. All work/labour is hazardous and harms the overall growth of the child.
4. There must be total abolition of child labour.
5. Any justification perpetuating the existence of child labour must be condemned.

Approach

Child labour is a burning issue in India. It is estimated that there are about 2 million children working in the so-called hazardous industries. If one were to define child labour as wage earning work alone the official estimates are around 12.6 million. Independent estimates, working on roughly the same definition have put the figures at around 40 million. However, if one were to define all children out of school as child labourers, the figure would be closer to 100 million. The MVF believes that the only way to tackle the problem of child labour is to harness the desire of parents for a better future for their children through education. It believes that the starting point for any programme to withdraw a child from work and enrol the kid in school is to promote the norm within the community that no child should work. Tackling the community implies not dealing with parents alone but the whole set of people including employers, opinion makers, elected local body representatives, community elders, local youths, teachers and so on. They ensure that the community leaders are supporting and sponsoring their programme, which then translates into a sense of community ownership in the programme. Their experiences in working with the parents has been very positive: almost all parents, even from the so called 'poorest' segment of the rural society, are not only keen on withdrawing their child from work and sending them to schools but are also willing to make whatever sacrifices in terms of money and time that this decision entails. Once a child is enrolled and shows some progress, parents have even sold off their cattle, sheep and so on, which were being looked after by the child and retained the child in school.

The MVF's approach is based on the assumption that child labour — and correspondingly being out of school — is intrinsically hazardous to the children's growth and well-being, given that they often work under inhuman conditions and sometimes in gross violation of basic human rights. Therefore the organization tries to ensure that every child attending school does so without any disruption until he or she completes class 10. It achieves this by community action which strives to remove all barriers. The MVF has developed the concept of a bridge course to prepare older children who missed out on formal schooling to be prepared for an age-appropriate class thus enabling them reintegrate into the formal system without any difficulty.

The organization follows a so-called 'area-based approach'. Unlike the 'target approach', this focuses on all children in an area within the 5–14 year age-group. Thus it covers all out-of-school children, withdraws them from work and mainstreams them into formal school. Simultaneously, it monitors every child in school and makes sure that they are retained in schools. It also takes up the twin responsibility of mobilizing and organizing communities for public action and puts pressure on the system to deliver services.

The organization does not act as a directly implementing agency but as a facilitator to the programme. It focuses attention on strengthening local institutions and thus all efforts at mobilization result in concrete actions like setting up forums, committees or pressure groups. Simultaneously, it aims to prepare the concerned public institutions to take care of children and their education in formal schools. In addition, the MVF also engages policy-makers to bring about systemic policy changes which address the needs of the children.

Background

The MVF was established in 1981 in memory of the educationist and historian, Professor Mamidipudi Venkatarangaiya. It started working on abolition of child labour in only three villages since 1991. The MVF has so far been able to withdraw 400,000 children from work in about 6,000 villages; and, with active involvement of local institution, implements the program directly in the Ranga Reddy, Nalgonda, Kurnool and Adilabad districts in Andhra Pradesh covering over 2,500 villages and in the city of Hyderabad.

Organizational Structure

As its operating model is as a facilitator, the organizational structure is decentralized. The governing body of the board of trustees with its chairperson is the apex body that meets once in a year to ratify programmes and to frame broad policy outlines of the MVF. It is assisted by the secretary-trustee who is in charge of the overall management of all the projects and the treasurer who is responsible for the financial management. Furthermore, the organization has a National Programme Advisory Committee (NPAC) and a Finance Advisory Committee (FAC) that meet at least once every six months where reports of all the activities and financial needs are presented. The institutions and the staff at the local area are fully independent in their daily work, and thus share full responsibility for planning, implementation and monitoring of the programme.

All the decisions taken are respected and even encouraged. They just act within a broad framework, that is, all members and staff of the MVF are subjected to the 'non-negotiables'; a charter of basic principles concerning the emancipation of children's rights. They are also guided by some organizational principles that emphasize respect for the field-level activist who is supposed to resolve conflicts in a non-violent fashion through debates and discussions and win over all stakeholders to support children's rights.

To coordinate the various projects and in order to be informed about the activities in the villages, there are regular meetings of the personnel at the different levels.

Members and Volunteers

Apart from 80,000 'volunteers' who are also paying members (75 cents/25 rupees), there are about 1,100 volunteers who work for the MVF.

Funding

Main Sponsors and Donors since Inception

MVFs main sponsors and donors are:

1. Ministries of Labour and HRD of the Government of India
2. The Government of Andhra Pradesh (World Bank Project—Velugu)
3. Child Rights and You—CRY
4. International Labour Organization—International Programme on the Elimination of Child Labour
5. European Union Consortium comprising of HIVOS, Concern, FNV, German Agro Action and PIN
6. National Child Labour Programme
7. National Council for Rural Institutes—NCRI
8. UNICEF

9.   United Nations Development Programme
10. UNDP/NORAD
11. The JRD Tata Trust
12. Sir Dorabji Tata Trust
13. Actionaid India
14. AusAid
15. Stiching Kinderpostzegels Nederland
16. Catholic Relief Services
17. Broadridge Financial Services
18. Axis Bank Foundation

In total, the core budget is $983,721 (42 million INR) and about $702,658 (30 million INR) is in the form of limited grants from some of the above-mentioned institutions and organizations.

Main Channels of Funding or Revenue Generation

The budget predominantly consists of the funding of the above-mentioned organizations or institutions; individual donors contribute only a little. Individual donations mainly consist of the 75 cents (25 INR) to join the forum.

On the website one can find several requests for funds like 'support social mobilization for child rights', 'support an education activist' or 'support a child'. Whereas the former only provides an appeal to join the movement against child labour and for children's right to education without the necessary and helpful details, the latter two include a brief description on how the money is used.

Publication/Transparency

The NGO has an annual report as well as progress reports for download on their website. An audit report is provided upon request.

Governance

The MVF interacts with the several local and district institutions on a regular as well as on an issue-specific basis.

Partnerships/Cooperation with other NGOs

The MVF is part of three nationwide networks: National Alliance for Right to Education (NAFRE, http://www.nafreindia.org/home.html), Campaign Against Child Labour (CACL, http://www.caclindia.org/) and Children's Right to Food (http://www.righttofoodindia.org/index.html). It is also part of a state-level network, the Andhra Pradesh Alliance for Right to Education. NAFRE fights for the right of equal education opportunities for all the children in India and for working opportunities for the adults. The network operates in more than 15 Indian states and encompasses approximately 2,400 voluntary organizations. The CACL not only focuses on the raising of public attention towards child labour, but also investigates the abuse of child labour and lobbies against it in the attempt to achieve their goal of total eradication of child labour. The network consists of more than 6,000 organizations fighting against child labour and includes trade unions and media agencies as well. The Children's Right to Food Campaign is an informal network of organizations and individuals with the belief that everyone has the right to appropriate nutrition. Thus, its aims to provide mid-day meals for people suffering from malnutrition. Further to this, the network wants to lobby for a National Employment Guarantee Act to help the people escape their current situation.

On a more local level it collaborates with other NGOs on an issue-specific basis, also debating operational questions. Furthermore, to implement their model, the MVF gives assistance to other NGOs at the local level, as well as to the government.

Communication Strategies

Main External Communication Channels and Strategies

The MVF uses a number of communication means to position their agenda in the public:

1. Events, cultural activities, speeches.
2. A printed newsletter in Telugu, the regional language of Andhra Pradesh.

3. Brochures, posters, emails, press releases.
4. One-to-one contact with key stakeholders in politics.
5. Public rallies.
6. Workshops with other NGOs.
7. Liaising with journalists to write small articles on MV Foundation's success stories (for example, portraits of the children, not directly about the NGO).
8. Even if the MVF does not use the internet that much for interaction with their stakeholders, one can find plenty of information on their website.

The MVF applies two different communication strategies. First they directly address the people at the grass-roots level to build awareness that every child should be in school. Second they try to demonstrate and convince political decision-makers that their approach adds value to society overall. It invites politicians and officials to visit their classes for older children who are catching up with the education they were not provided at younger age. Following the visit, the Foundation tries to stay in touch and contacts them regularly. It is a step-by-step approach, starting at the community level to convince local politicians and opinion leaders, so their messages spread by word-of-mouth to the state and the national level. In addition, the MVF invites other NGOs from all over the world to see its work. In 2003, the MVF was awarded with the Magsaysay Award, the 'Asian Nobel Peace Prize'.

Main Internal Communication Channels and Strategies

The MVF's main internal communication channels are mobile and landline telephone, email, personal meetings as well as the sharing of formal minutes of meetings. Due to this decentralization, the MVF does not have many formalized communication structures but quite a number of informal meetings and a special kind of programme review mechanism. Every local unit meets regularly to share their experiences and, at the district level, delegates from the local units report on their experiences and challenges. Furthermore the MVF has several core groups with regular core group review meetings: once every fifteen days at the local level, once a month at the district level and once every three months at the programme and national levels.

Research

In attempting to convince politicians, the MVF does a lot of research. A number of research reports are available for download on their website. Often, outcomes of field studies and surveys are published in the media to provide evidence supporting MVF's objectives. The MVF is supported by a Delhi-based research organization, the 'HAQ—Centre for Child Rights' (http://www.haqcrc.org/). The Centre provides valuable research on statistical issues such as the number of discussions in parliament dealing with issues related to children and also provides insights into the situation of child labourers, such as those working in mines. All of its research is accessible in print for other individuals and organizations in order to achieve the biggest impact.

Campaigns

The MVF equates an 'out of school child' with the phenomenon of child labour and advocates for the adoption of this definition as a benchmark in policy and law alike. It runs permanent campaigns concerning the total abolition of child labour and children's right to education and food. These campaigns have come in the form of the Right to Education Bill, Total Abolition of Child Labour (http://www.mvfindia.in/totalabolition_ofchildlabour.htm), Children's Right to Food (http://www.mvfindia.in/childrensrighttofood.htm) and the Stop Child Labour Campaign (http://www.mvfindia.in/stopchild_labourcampaign.htm). But they also campaign on specific issues through petitioning, courts, protests in front of government buildings, at public forums, and so on.

Assessment of Campaigns

The MVF has two criteria for evaluating the success of its campaigns:

1. How does the government react? 'If the policy has changed, then we think this is a success' (Venkat Reddy, www.mvfindia.in).
2. It is a success when another local based institution is built: 'Every campaign should lead to an institutional building of the MV Foundation' (Venkat Reddy, www.mvfindia.in).

Advertising

The MVF does not have a special advertising or marketing strategy.

Information

Interested people can find a wealth of information and documents pertaining to the organization and on the subject of child labour by visiting the MVF website, which also provides a wealth of information on related topics and other frequently asked questions.

Special Feature: Volunteers

Volunteers are crucial for the MVF and the Foundation strongly incorporates a large number of volunteers into all areas of its daily work. There are two types of volunteers:

1. Child rights protection forum volunteers: These people are true volunteers as they invest their time in the MVF without any payment. For a lifetime fee of 75 cents (25 INR) they join the Child Rights Protection Forum, an independent part of the MVF.
2. Paid volunteers: In contrast to the true volunteers there are about 1,100 people who work for the NGO in paid positions.

All the MVF volunteers are recruited through a particular strategy. For example, if the MV Foundation visits a village aiming at mobilization, it identifies people who then start to work slowly with the NGO. All volunteers start at the grassroots level, but improve their skills over time and become experts. On demand by the volunteers, the Foundation provides them special training and workshops. From here, the MV Foundation's volunteers graduate to take on new assignments and roles in the organization and their capacities are enhanced. They work in all areas and are responsible for all children in a village.

Contact

M V Foundation
201, Narayan Apartments
West Marredpally
Secunderabad–500026
Andhra Pradesh, India.
Phone: +91 (40) 2780-1320
Fax: +91 (40) 2780-8808
E-mail: mvfindia@gmail.com
Website: http://www.mvfindia.in/index.asp

Chapter Six

Strategic Research

*How many things are looked upon as quite
impossible until they have been actually affected?*

Pliny the Elder

THE TOOLS introduced in this section help us understand the dynamics in a respective policy field. It helps in scoping and quantifying the issue and facilitates in the collection of evidence that you are making the right case. In order to get attention, raise awareness and trigger a discussion, it is important that one can prove that the problem is continuing to grow and needs to be addressed by certain actions directed towards policy change.

Questions answered in this section are:

1. What are the dynamics in your specific policy field? How does the market work? How successful will you potentially be in positioning yourself? This requires an understanding of the competition and entry barriers in your field.

2. What do you bring to the table? Where and what are your strengths and weaknesses? Tools introduced here are SWOT analysis and competitor analysis.

3. How can you quantify the issue? The tools introduced are primary and secondary research tools like desk research and survey research.

4. How can you show that there is a correlation between the issue and specific public structures or social practices? The tool introduced here is statistical analysis.

PRIMARY AND SECONDARY RESEARCH

The happiness of your life depends on the quality of your thoughts.

Marcus Aurelius Antoninus

Research provides the basis for coming up with fact-based strategic decisions. It is the flesh that one puts around your strategic skeleton. A good researcher has a key skill that is absolutely needed in your strategic undertaking: not only to know where the information nuggets are, but also to separate the relevant facts from the superfluous data, contextualize them, synthesize them and apply them.

Probably more than once one gets lost in the ocean of information and data of the worldwide web, drowning in trillions of websites! These days, where the web provides a wealth of information to everyone, it is impossible to successfully compete by just knowing more. You need to know better and differentiate through synthesis and analysis. The key skill of a knowledge worker today is to distinguish the relevant from the irrelevant and reduce a complex problem into small, workable chunks. So a good researcher is by definition a strategic researcher, applying analytical skills and, of course, common sense to the question to be researched.

There are basically two ways of doing research, depending on the degree of data availability.

1. Secondary Research: Retrieving information from existing sources. These can be freely available on the web, accessible at a public or university library or through paid sources. For almost every existing industry segment, industry analysts offer their services to provide you with tailored data points concerning the business. Through secondary research, you always look into the past.

2. Primary Research: When secondary information does not exist, one has to generate it through interviews. In the following chapters we will look into survey research in detail. The main advantage of primary research is that one is able to make assumptions about the future.

In primary research, there are two approaches which can be distinguished as shown in Figure 6.1.

FIGURE 6.1
Differences between Qualitative and Quantitative Research

Qualitative	Quantitative
Provides depth of understanding	Measures level of occurrence
Asks 'Why?'	Asks 'How many?' and 'How often?'
Studies motivations	Studies actions
Is subjective	Is objective
Enables discovery	Provides proof
Is exploratory	Is definitive
Allows insights into behaviour, trends, and so on	Measures level of actions, trends, and so on
Interprets	Describes

Source: Cabanero-Verzosa (2003).

There are a number of tools available to conduct research of both types. Figure 6.2 provides an overview of the research tools and techniques.

MARKET AND ORGANIZATIONAL ANALYSIS

Now you can start positioning your organization. To understand the market, three tools are available in the commercial world which can provide a lot of direction for the non-profit world:

FIGURE 6.2
Research Value Chain

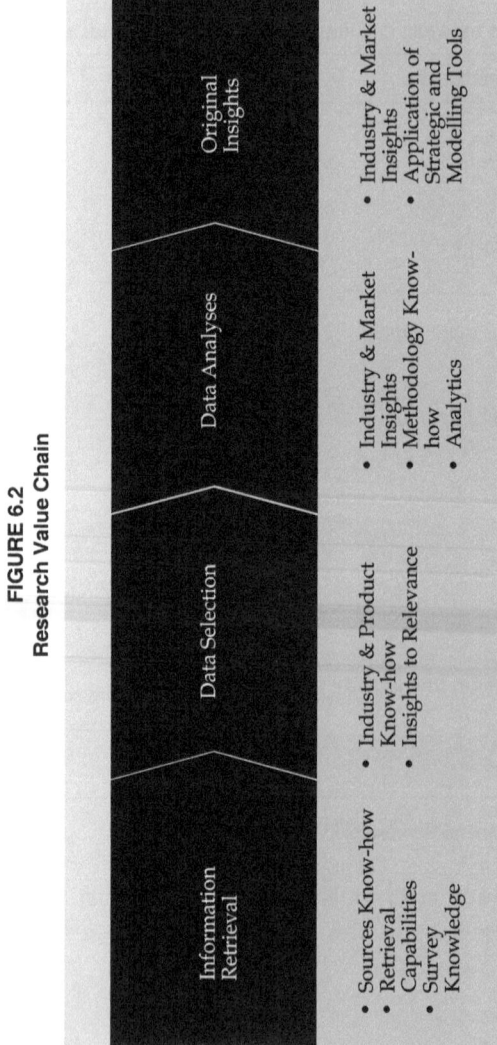

	Information Retrieval	Data Selection	Data Analyses	Original Insights
Capabilities	• Sources Know-how • Retrieval Capabilities • Survey Knowledge	• Industry & Product Know-how • Insights to Relevance	• Industry & Market Insights • Methodology Know-how • Analytics	• Industry & Market Insights • Application of Strategic and Modelling Tools

Source: Developed by the authors.

1. Industry Analysis
2. Competitive Analysis
3. SWOT Analysis

INDUSTRY ANALYSIS

> *Chaos often breeds life, when order breeds habit.*
>
> Henry Brooks Adams

Industry analysis (see Figure 6.3) is a key activity to understand the drivers, dynamics and potential in the industry in which one is operating. It might sound funny to describe the NGO sector as an industry, but, in fact, the sector shows similar dynamics which apply to the for profit sector. Also, it has grouped itself around different policy fields; for example health, welfare, youth, and so on, similar to the profit world which defines their products and services, customer groups and distribution networks accordingly. The main difference is that in the commercial world the objective is to maximize revenue, whereas in the non-profit sector it is the maximization of value for their cause. Similar to the commercial world, NGOs 'compete' for sponsorship, attention and influence. As in a profit seeking entity, 'rivalry' – another word for competition – helps NGOs as well to define their unique value that they want to bring to heir constituents. Consequently both for-profit organizations and NGOs competition provides better products and services!

Industry analysis will give an indication what it takes to establish oneself as a player in either a commercial or not-for-profit market.

Michael E. Porter identified the following forces:

The Rivalry among Existing Sellers in the Market

What is important here is the number and capability of your competition – if there are many competitors, and they offer equally attractive products and services, then one will most likely have little power. If no one else can do what you do, then you are well

FIGURE 6.3
Porter's Five Forces

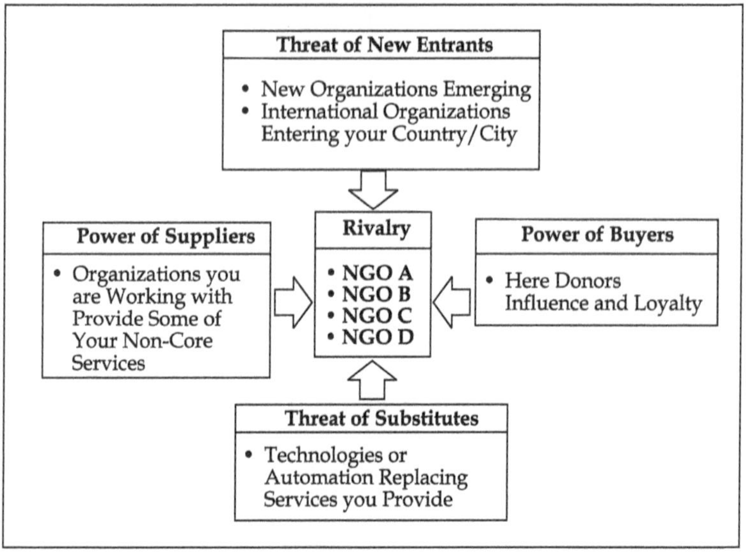

Threat of New Entrants
- New Organizations Emerging
- International Organizations Entering your Country/City

Power of Suppliers
- Organizations you are Working with Provide Some of Your Non-Core Services

Rivalry
- NGO A
- NGO B
- NGO C
- NGO D

Power of Buyers
- Here Donors Influence and Loyalty

Threat of Substitutes
- Technologies or Automation Replacing Services you Provide

Source: Porter (2008).

positioned. This is obviously not the case if your competition offers the same products and services at the same price or better quality for a lower price. In reference to our example this might mean that the perceived value of one's services to the community will influence donors to either support you or somebody else.

The Power Exerted by the Customers in the Market

Here one should ask oneself how easy or difficult it is for customers to put pressure on pricing. The answer to this question is driven by the number of buyers, and thus, the importance of each individual buyer to your business, and the cost to them of switching from your products and services to those of someone else. An NGO is also dependent on an acceptance of its services. If the number of recipients is small and they have other options to obtain better services with lower costs to themselves, then they might switch to another NGO or to another business.

The Impact of the Suppliers on the Sellers

Here one assesses how easy or difficult it is for suppliers to drive up prices. This is determined by the number of suppliers, the uniqueness of their product or service, and consequently, their control over the seller. Furthermore, it looks at the potential cost of changing the supplier. The fewer the supplier choices that are available, the more one depends on them and the more powerful they become. As an NGO offering a portfolio of different services one might end up being very dependent on a supply of certain services crucial to one's business. Assuming that POCA partners with an NGO offering health services crucial to the NGO's portfolio, a change in pricing or expectation might be threatening to the NGO.

The Potential Threat of New Sellers Entering the Market

Position and power is also affected by the ability of organizations to enter the same market and/or policy field. If it costs little to enter your market and compete effectively, if there are few economies of scale in place, or if one has little protection for one's key assets, then new competitors can quickly emerge and weaken one's position. If organizations can easily enter the same policy field, the competition for donations and public attention increases, thereby negatively affecting one's ability to initiate policy change.

The Threat of Substitute Products Becoming Available in the Market

This is affected by the ability of one's customers to find a different way of doing what you provide.

For example, if an NGO provides a specific psychological counselling programme tailored to the needs of children with HIV/AIDS, a competitor might supplement a similar counselling programme with legal aid.

COMPETITIVE ANALYSIS

The reasonable man adapts himself to the world; the unreasonable one persists in trying to adapt the world to him. Therefore, all progress depends on the unreasonable man.

George Bernard Shaw

Competitive intelligence will help to understand better who is doing what in the market place. Depending on the number of organizations in the same policy field as well as the likeliness of new entrants or substitutes, it is recommended that this exercise is done on a regular basis. Large organizations have whole departments doing nothing else but investigating its competitors' activities. The reason for this is that in our fast moving economy — both for profit and non-profit — it can make a significant difference to the success of your undertaking if you can identify an opportunity to attract donations first. The 'first mover advantage' may be the key differentiator. The process one needs to follow is quite simple, but you need to make sure that research is done thoroughly and thoughtfully. Figure 6.4 illustrates an approach for executing competitive intelligence research.

As a result of this exercise you will gain an insightful competitive landscape which will help to understand where an organization is positioned. The best sources to get an understanding of the players in the same field are:

1. Associations: In the NGO sector especially, there are a number of umbrella organizations representing the interests of a variety of institutions; typically they have a fairly good understanding of the market.
2. Press searches: There are a number of paid sources like Factiva or Reuters where you can search a wealth of newspapers and magazines for relevant articles. Moreover, many newspapers have fairly good online archives theses days where you can get relevant information for free.
3. Web searches: The web is — despite the danger of getting lost in information overload — an ocean full of valuable nuggets that can help you understand your competitive environment.

FIGURE 6.4
Approach to Competitive Intelligence

Objectives & Key Questions	Identify Competitors	Profiling	Positioning	Gain Strategic Insights
• What do we want to achieve with competitive intelligence, e.g formulating an USP, identifying threats, considering competitive responses	• Create and validate list of potential competitors • Consider new entrants and potential substitutes	• Collect information on competitors through secondary sources and/or primary research (survey, interviews, focus groups)	• Create parameters for comparison • Get an understanding of competitive positioning of others and yourself	• Develop and discuss implications for your organization as per findings of your SWOT analysis

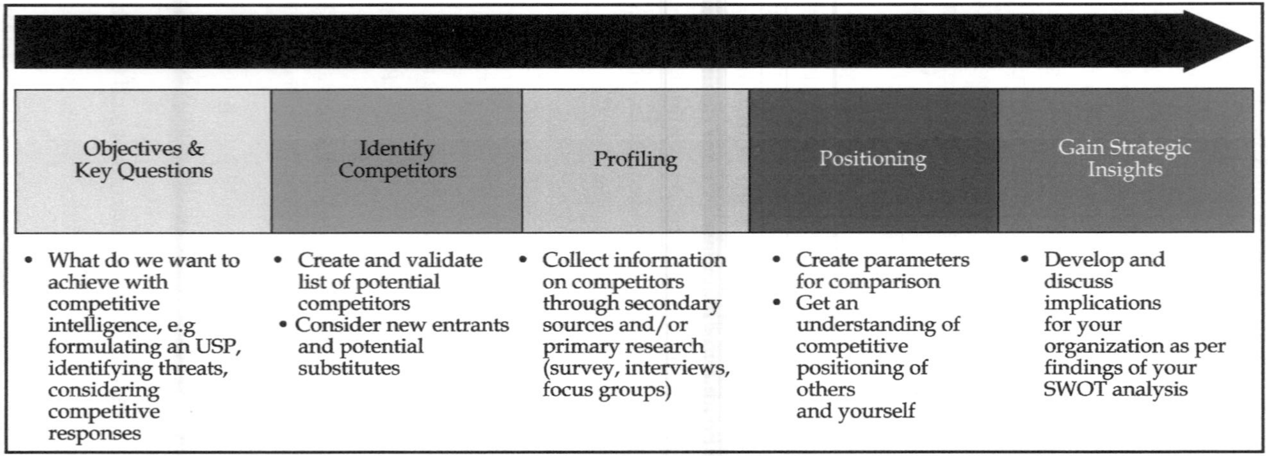

Source: Developed by the authors.

Use the technique of 'snowballing', that is, going from one page to another to understand more. Apart from Google and Yahoo, go to places like Google Scholar for the academic side of things as well. Do not forget checking blogs as they are a very powerful source of first hand, up-to-date information.

4. Primary interviews with experts: You might like to talk to experts on the sector in which you are interested; these experts might come from ministries, international organizations or academia. A number of organizations such as the UN or Duke University have created databases with lists of NGOs by policy field.

It is critical that not-for-profit organizations do not bring the same vision in the same way to the same audience in a specific policy field. Differentiations as well as the communication are key for its success. In combination with your industry analysis, you should now be able to get a view of your position as well as of the opportunities ahead. In order to streamline this understanding, another kind of framework is available: the SWOT analysis: Strength–Weakness–Opportunities–Threats

SWOT Analysis

> *Drive thy business; let it not drive thee.*
>
> Benjamin Franklin

The next most important step in your analysis is to look at your own strengths and weaknesses, opportunities and threats. One can differentiate between:

1. Internal factors: The strengths and weaknesses within the organization.
2. External factors: The opportunities and threats presented by the external environment.

It is recommended to draw a table (see Table 6.1) to better understand the overall fit of an organization:

TABLE 6.1
Example for a SWOT Analysis

Strengths–Action: Build and leverage (Key advantage, unique resources, key strength)	Weaknesses–Action: Remedy or exit (Areas for improvement)
Examples:	Examples:
1. Image and brand 2. Motivated employees 3. Large numbers of supporters	1. Poor infrastructure 2. Leadership continuity 3. Efficiency
Opportunities–Action: Prioritize, optimize (Changes in the market providing new opportunities)	Threats–Action: Counter (Competitor activities, substitute offerings, regulation)
Examples:	Examples:
1. Changes in regulations empower NGOs in this policy field 2. Tax reform in favour of more donations in this policy field	1. New NGO emerging in this policy field 2. Economic conditions

Source: Developed by the authors.

Based on their research, the industry and the competitive analysis and the SWOT analysis POCA has gained the following understanding:

- There are numerous NGOs in India looking at children and a large number looking into HIV/AIDS. None are combining the two policy fields and addressing the specific needs of children.
- The industry analysis has helped POCA understand that despite the fact that they are the only ones combining the two issues, organizations and health experts in the ministry that they deal with expect very high levels of expertise with regards to the subject, HIV/AIDS.
- POCA understands that it is well positioned in the community but lack the breath and depth of networks in those two complex policy fields.

Having finalized this exercise, one knows where one stands and can invest in ones strengths and address the challenges.

The Young European Federalists can be considered a best practice in market and industry analysis. Driven by the objective to expand within and outside Europe, they are trying to equip their new members with knowledge and tools to understand the environment they are operating in.

BEST PRACTICE CASE STUDY: YOUNG EUROPEAN FEDERALISTS—JEF

Mission/Vision

The Young European Federalists (Junge Europäische Föderalisten – JEF) is a non-governmental, non-party based political organization of young people from all over Europe, who share a vision of a united, federal and democratic Europe. JEF brings together people on the local, regional, national and European levels to campaign for a federal Europe based on the values of peace, democracy and the rule of law.

Approach

JEF pursues a decision-making approach based on 'federalist' principles. According to those subsidiary principles, all decisions in a society shall be made at the societal level of most relevance and should not be made at a higher level than necessary. The underlying assumption is that each individual should have the right to exercise maximum influence in all matters which concern him or her. The institutional power structure of a society should support the idea that the authority to deal with and solve an issue rests with those affected by it. In addition JEF claims that the principles of democracy have to be embedded in all spheres of life: in the workplace, in residential communities and in educational institutions. To promote the European Federation, JEF organises international seminars, trainings, conferences, campaigns, street activities and lobbying activities.

Background

JEF was established as a non-profit association in 1949 in Brussels, Belgium. It is an umbrella organization combining entities of member states on the national level.

FIGURE 6.5
JEF Organizational Structure

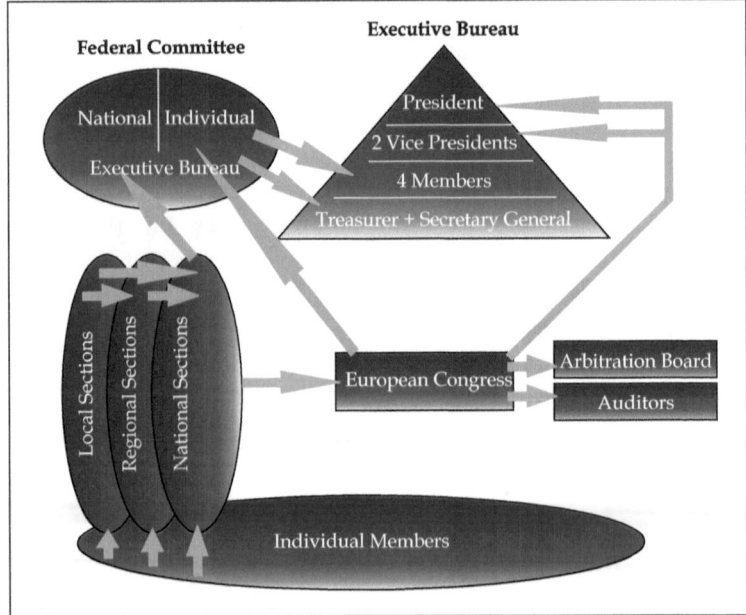

Source: http://www.jef.eu/ (Accessed in August 2008).

The organization is run through a congress, a federal committee and an executive bureau (see Figure 6.5).

The congress is the supreme body of JEF and includes delegates elected by JEF national sections. The congress meets every two years to define the general political direction of the NGO as well as to promote its policies in specific areas. Furthermore it elects the president for a mandate of two years, the two vice-presidents and involves the directly elected members of the federal committee.

The federal committee, which meets twice a year, is the main decision-making political body of JEF. It has the operational authority over the work of the association and defines the policies between the semi-annual congress meetings and coordinates the activities among the sections. It is formed by one representative of each national section of JEF as well as approximately 20 members elected directly by the congress. Each of the 20 elected

members is also responsible for one specific and clearly defined area of JEF activity or policy focus. This allows JEF to represent both its national sections and the European level according to their principle of federalism. The federal committee elects the secretary general, the treasurer and the executive bureau whose administration is also controlled by the committee. The executive bureau meets at least four times a year and is responsible for the management of the organization. It includes the president, the two vice-presidents, at least four members elected by the federal committee, the secretary general, and the treasurer. It has to implement the decisions and is responsible for ensuring that JEF's campaigns and activities are being run efficiently and effectively.

The five members of the arbitration board, the 'internal clearinghouse' are elected by the congress and function to settle statutory conflicts between members, JEF sections, and the statutory bodies of the JEF.

Most Important Stakeholder Groups

JEF's most important stakeholder groups are its members, as they ensure debate and innovation. The members are the key resource for the achievement of international democracy through the establishment of federal systems in Europe and across the world. This is considered more important than the money they donate.

Members and Volunteers

Apart from the secretary general everybody is a volunteer. JEF has approximately 30,000 members and volunteers in more than 30 countries.

Funding

In general, the organization's funding is project based. JEF–Europe receives financial support from the European Commission in the form of administrative grants, the Council of Europe and individual

donors. Funds are also raised through the JEF website where the organization's bank details can be found if one wants to submit funds. Another option for supporting JEF is to post an advertisement in their print magazine *The New Federalist* or on the online version (www.thenewfederalist.eu).

Main Sponsors and Donors

JEF gets financial support in terms of administrative grants from the European Commission, the different projects grants from institutions, private trusts, governments, individual donations and membership fees. Fees contribute 30 to 40 per cent of the overall budget.

Networking

Official sections are located not only in EU countries, but also throughout Europe. Thus, you can find JEF in Albania, Austria, Belgium, Bosnia and Herzegovina, Bulgaria, Croatia, Czech Republic, Denmark, Finland, France, Greece, Germany, Hungary, Italy, Latvia, Lithuania, Macedonia, Malta, Moldova, Montenegro, Norway, Poland, Portugal, Romania, Serbia, Slovakia, Slovenia, Spain, Sweden, Switzerland and the UK.

JEF–Europe is a member of three larger networks, the European Movement International, the World Federalists' Movement and the European Youth Forum. The European Movement's main focus centres upon influencing political, social and cultural arenas within the framework of the European Civil Society. The World Federalists' Movement brings together organizations and individuals that support the establishment of a global federal system. The European Youth Forum tries to empower young citizens of the EU to participate in the shaping of European policies and to change the given circumstances for living. Apart from that, the JEF collaborates in specific projects with the Union of European Federalists and the Youth Politicals, which are the youth sections of the European political parties.

Communication Strategies

JEF has a pointedly targeted message and follows several channels in its communication strategy. Because JEF has a federal structure it disseminates messages and information as well as potential areas of concern through its sub-sections (from the European level to the national and regional level). Its strategy to cope with the multi-level communication and reach 'ordinary people' is, to simplify its message which is to convey the information by linking specific policies and issues of the EU to people's quotidian lives (such as mentioning the Euro or better ways of transportation, among others). In that way the message becomes clearer and more accessible.

To further disseminate information, JEF tries to involve as many people as possible from outside the organization. It mainly works with young people, mostly students, but also experts and professionals, who are invited to its seminars and workshops. Furthermore, JEF is involved at the European level, initiating activities like lobbying or pan-European campaigns, which take place simultaneously in all its member sections. A very successful example involving decision-makers was the Galaxy Europe campaign where people from all over Europe could approach the Member of European Parliament (MEP) directly and put forth their concerns. At the end of the campaign, all the people were called upon to nominate the best MEP. Other strategies involve directly addressing the parliament. They also hold international seminars in different countries and invite politicians at the national level.

Main External Communication Channels

One of the most important communication strategies is campaigning on the streets, where JEF tries to reach out to as many different people in a short time. It also works a lot in Brussels with press releases targeted at the European media. The NGO not only focuses on a federal Europe and closer cooperation between JEF members across all states, but also follows the political agenda from a pan-European perspective and tries to lobby and comment on up-to-date issues. To keep their supporters informed, JEF also

publicizes their press and media releases on their official website, another communication channel. On the website, a particularly important section is the public forum where people can discuss any matter relating Europe and JEF.

Other crucial communication channels are customized emails disseminated through direct mailing to several online group lists with different information needs, for example, 'JEF Active' to inform people and to establish regular contact between JEF and its supporters; the different sub-sites of the various projects such as 'Speak up Europe'; petitions; Facebook and the newsletters (both internal and external). There are English, French and German versions of the newsletter which can be subscribed to online.

JEF publishes its own magazine *The New Federalist*. Both the online and the print version of the magazine are published three times a year and contain essays and analyses on European issues written by JEF members. *The New Federalist* is also a publication where interested people and JEF supporters can learn about upcoming JEF events and read reports by participants of the various international conferences and seminars organized by the NGO. The print version is also distributed to JEF sections and among the European Parliament while the online version of the magazine also serves as a forum for discussion.

Main Internal Communication Channels

JEF mainly uses the direct way of communication, that is, the top-down approach, disseminating information from the European to the national level, from the national to the regional level, from the regional to the local level and from the local level to the individual. It tries to use this direct way as much as possible, because it is the best way to address and engage people and works much better than mass mailings. However, daily communication is done via email, telephone, and personal contact. They do provide newsletters, mailing and discussion lists as well. Furthermore, the website provides an exclusive area for JEF members who are required to login using a password in order to access it. Within the executive board there are different members who are responsible for a specific sub-section. Although the general secretary is always there to assist, every sub-section has this regular personal contact with its specific board member. To ensure the flow of communication and information, these executive board members update other members in regular meetings.

Research on Communication

The NGO has established long-term relationships with its partners and therefore focuses on improving existing communication tools rather than coming up with completely new ways of communicating. However, depending on the development of the organization's environment, the NGO tries to adapt new strategies such as using Facebook as a fast way of putting a 'face to the name' and linking up people in an way that is both effective and highly appreciated. Suggestions for new communication strategies are developed by the working group for branding.

Campaigns

Basically JEF tries to campaign locally as much as possible, while simultaneously campaigning in Brussels in order to reach the politicians or other stakeholders. Mobilization is of crucial importance for campaigning, as JEF has to motivate and enable the sub-sections to take part in their (pan-European) campaigns. It organizes dramatic international campaigns that take place at the same time all over Europe. One example has been gagging statues, in order to bring a European dimension to local events and to motivate people to take part in its campaigns. The latest campaign, 'I Want My Flag Back' was initiated to raise awareness about the Reform Treaty and the European Council meeting for the official signing of the Reform Treaty on 13 and 14 December 2007. Within the scope of this campaign many activities, debates and street actions were organized and arranged throughout the different sub-units of JEF. The major idea was to show all the stakeholders that the members want to see a European Union united under one flag and, maybe also, with one anthem. Thus the idea was to put posters with the European flag all over the cities where JEF operates in order to attract media awareness.

Recently, JEF carried out several campaigns such as 'Galaxy Europe' in 2006, the 'YES!' campaign in 2005 and 'Give Europe a Face!' in 2004–2005. The main objective of the former was to promote the European Parliament and bring the work of the MEPs closer to young citizens. In 2005, JEF actively campaigned in favour of the European Constitution. By building a coalition of a variety of representatives from different sectors of civil society the 'YES!' campaign focused on credibility and legitimacy of the pan-European vision. In addition, the collaboration generated the momentum for a trans-national series of events where citizens can become familiar with the European Constitution and get a flavour of its importance. The objectives of the 'Give Europe a Face' campaign can be explained as an attempt at fostering the idea of European citizenship by spreading the idea that there is more that unites young people in Europe than what separates them.

As it is difficult to campaign for the idea of Europe, JEF rather initiates long-term campaigns. Nevertheless, in case a new innovation or change occurs, they can also campaign for these specific current issues. Furthermore, JEF focuses on creating synergies between the different communication strategies and channels; in practice, they campaign at the local level, initiate events, use the website and involve their partner organizations.

Assessment of Campaigns

A separate group within the NGO, the 'Working group Branding', consisting of people who are experts in PR, design, and so forth, is responsible for evaluating JEFs efforts to gain more visibility in order to improve both their internal and external communications. In general, the NGO uses survey techniques, distributing evaluation forms after a certain campaign, seminar or workshop so that it can gather information about its performance.

Advertising/Marketing

The most successful tools are press releases where JEF tries to be as fast as possible, innovative and provocative. Another strategy is to refer to the NGOs strength and size to advertise the organization. Gaining attention at the national and local level is crucial for JEF's advertising strategy. At these levels they also use events, press conferences and the like. The JEF online shop provides post cards, brochures, leaflets and t-shirts that can be ordered.

Source: http://www.jef.eu/ (Accessed in August 2008).

Special Feature

Information and Documents on the Website

The JEF website has the unique feature of an 'info pool' which helps in setting up a new group, getting the financials right and plan an event in the right manner. Here, new groups find everything they need to get started. The communication section is providing tools and guidelines for members on how to sell the idea of JEF as well as how to deal with the media.

Source: http://www.jef.eu/ (Accessed in August 2008).

Specifically, there are toolkits on campaigning, (in particular the golden rules for a successful campaign), street actions, international seminars, panel discussions and lobbying. The sub-site 'communication' provides guidelines for internal and external communication of an association (how to organize regular meetings or develop a membership magazine) as well as methods and advice for talking to the media and writing a press release.

One can find a template for a newsletter and an example for a press release: 'Presenting JEF to the World', practical guidelines for launching a website or creating a flyer as well as information on how to set up a SWOT analysis for analysing a single JEF section and improving future work.

Contact

JEF–Europe Secretariat
Chausse de Wavre 214d, 1050 Brussels
Phone: +32 (0)2 5120053, Fax: +32 (0)2 6269501
E-mail: info@jef.eu
Website: http://www.jef.eu

STATISTICAL ANALYSIS

If you can't measure it, you can't manage it.

Peter Drucker

In order to initiate policy change it is absolutely critical to show evidence between specific public policies or social practices and the issues you like to resolve. Statistical analysis can help to show the correlation between two events and to provide evidence that one event affects the other. For example, suppose that the decision to give out condoms for free has resulted in a decrease of reported HIV cases in a specific area. However, statistics show nothing but a relationship between two data points and one has logic to ascribe meaning to them. Statistically, one can show the correlation between the shoe size of a CEO and the performance of a company. These days, numerous tools for statistical analysis exist, the most famous one being Microsoft Excel®. But let me give you some basics about averages, growth rates and how to draw conclusions from data. Statistics is a science which requires lots of time and experience in order to become an expert. Some tips will help you to structure your arguments better.

The Average

'Lying with averages' is widely used. A well-known example is that women are said to be incapable of doing specific types of work, because their physical constitution is less strong than men. Whereas this is true on average, the spread in a female population is so broad that it does not make sense to exclude them from certain roles based on that argument.

There are three types of averages:

1. Mean: is the arithmetic average.
2. Median: occupies the middle position in a ranked series and is not affected by outliers. With even number of observations, add the two central values and divide by 2.
3. Mode: is the average of cases that you find most often.

Applying it to our examples, the usage of a specific type can make a big difference. If you wanted to understand the average number of cases of children with HIV/AIDS in India, you look at the distribution by state (see Table 6.2).

TABLE 6.2
Averages

State	Number of Persons Affected
State 1	5,000
State 2	7,200
State 3	7,800
State 4	9,600
State 5	9,600
State 6	9,600
State 7	10,800
State 8	12,000
State 9	120,000
Total number of cases (SUM)	191,600

Source: Developed by the authors.

If one would take the arithmetic average by dividing the sum by the number of states, the result would be almost 22,000 cases per state. This, however, would be an unfair representation, as the number of cases in State 9 is much higher than in others. In our case one would choose the median of 9,600 to make a statement about the average number of cases by state.

One other important thing to remember is not to average averages. If you have the average number of cases in two countries, do not sum the two averages up and divide them by two — you will get a wrong result. To get a fair representation, you need to sum up all cases from the two groups and calculate the average.

Growth Rates

POCA would like to report on the growth rates over four years in a specific state (see Table 6.3):

TABLE 6.3
Growth Rates

Year	Number of Cases	YoY Growth
2000	100	
2001	120	20%
2002	108	–10%
2003	108	0%

Source: Porter (1980).

The number of cases has grown from 100 to 120 between 2000 and 2001 and then stays at 108 in 2002 and 2003. If you calculate the growth year by year, you would see 20 per cent from 2000 to 2001, –10 per cent from 2001 to 2002 and then 0 per cent between 2002 and 2003. To calculate the growth rate over the years, one should use the Compound Annual Growth Rate (CAGR). The formula is simple:

(Value in the last year/Value in the first year)^(1/number of years) –1.

In our case it would be:

$(108/100)^{(1/3)} - 1 = 2.6$ per cent

POCA can now report that the number of cases has on average grown by 2.6 per cent per year.

Drawing Conclusions

The most important thing is that you derive the right conclusions from your data. Look at this example: 'For each kilometre travelled, three times more people die on trains than on airplanes.'

So flying is remarkably safer than going by train. The underlying statistic is correct, but is it a fair conclusion? Is the basis of the comparison fair? If you want to compare the security of a travel modes, isn't the time you spend within a travel mode more relevant than the distance travelled? If one changes the parameter from kilometres to travel duration, then the result is reversed. Then the statement would look as follows: For each hour travelled, three times more people die on airplanes than on trains – a completely different picture.

This example shows how much difference the representation of data can make. As you are using data to provide factual evidence for the case you want to make, it is very important to get it right. The most important question is the significance of the data present. Question: Is the difference between 10 per cent and 20 per cent significant? And the answer is: it depends – on your sample size.

A real life example illustrates the case:

The employee survey shows that 10 per cent of POCA's managers were satisfied last year, whereas 20 per cent are satisfied this year. Is this difference of 10 percentage points of any significance or is it a chance result? If you have 30 managers in total, a change of 10 per cent in employee satisfaction can't be considered significant. The picture would change if you have 100 managers in total.

In general, the sample size and standard deviation influence statistical significance. The larger the sample is, the less differential is needed for the values to be statistically significant. The lower the standard deviation, the higher is the significance. Thus, eliminating outlying information on either end of the scale from a dataset can 'make' significance. The example showing the distribution by state gives you a good example. Here, the large number in State 9 is an outlier changing the significance of your data. However, one has to be careful with 'statistical significance'. It does not always mean that a result is of practical relevance or irrelevance.

SURVEY RESEARCH

> *'Why' and 'How' are words so important that*
> *they cannot be too often used.*

Napoleon Bonaparte

Surveys or primary research can help in a number of situations such as:

1. When secondary data does not exist.
2. When one wants to understand and analyse customers' behaviours, needs and/or attitudes.
3. When one wants to get an idea about opinions and attitudes of key stakeholders in your ecosystem (donors, employees, management trustees, public administration representatives, politicians, the media, and so on).
4. When one wants to track the impact of your political communication efforts ante post and/or to predict the result of an election.

There are two different types of research surveys with two distinct objectives: the qualitative surveys aim to explore and analyse attitudes and/or behaviours while the quantitative surveys aim to measure the importance of attitudes and/or behaviours. Qualitative research uses an open-ended, narrative-based, observation approach to interviewing people and might be used with small sample sizes. The main tools used are interview guides (one-to-one interviews) or discussion guides (focus groups) that include only open-ended questions. Qualitative interviews are usually conducted in-person, that is, face to face, but may also be conducted by phone. Focus groups are usually conducted face to face (2–3 hour meetings of 8–10 participants in a single location) but also virtually (online focus groups and bulletin boards). The outcomes are directionally representative findings, giving in-depth insights into attitudes or opinions which help us understand the interviewees' view on the general direction of the market, in society or an organization. Quantitative research is a focused, repeatable approach using a standardized questionnaire with a large majority of closed questions. Typically, we use this for large sample sizes like opinion polls or customer satisfaction surveys. The data collection can be conducted via face-to-face interviews, phone, the web or mail. The outcome will be statistically significant results, that is, results that can be extrapolated to the population surveyed.

A survey is a very structured approach and it is necessary to be 'purist' on sampling and questionnaire design (see Figure 6.6) to ensure that you get the expected results.

Sampling

Sampling makes all the difference. The following example illustrates this:

Married men live longer! The mortality risk of married men is 11 per cent, while for bachelors it is 23 per cent. These numbers are true and not made up, but is it a fair conclusion? The trick: 'preselected sample'. Men who married tend to be wealthier and healthier than those who did not marry. So, it is not that marriage extends your life, but that the average women tend to choose the more promising candidate!

This example clarifies that the sample has to be a fair representation of the overall population of a given population cluster or organizations you want to survey. The best way to achieve that is through random sampling, meaning that every respondent has the same chance to be included into the sample. Concretely, one would randomly choose names from the overall population of individuals to be surveyed. How many would one choose to survey? This depends on the overall size of the population, the size of the sub-groups within that population. For example, the German electorate of 60 million people is surveyed using a sample size of only 800 people. In addition to the sample size the success of the prediction is related to the fact that people are directly surveyed at the site where they cast their vote.

The recommended minimal sample size for quantitative analysis is 100 interviews and no quantitative analysis can be conducted on a sample below 30 interviews. Samples below 30 interviews usually are used for qualitative research.

FIGURE 6.6
Survey Process

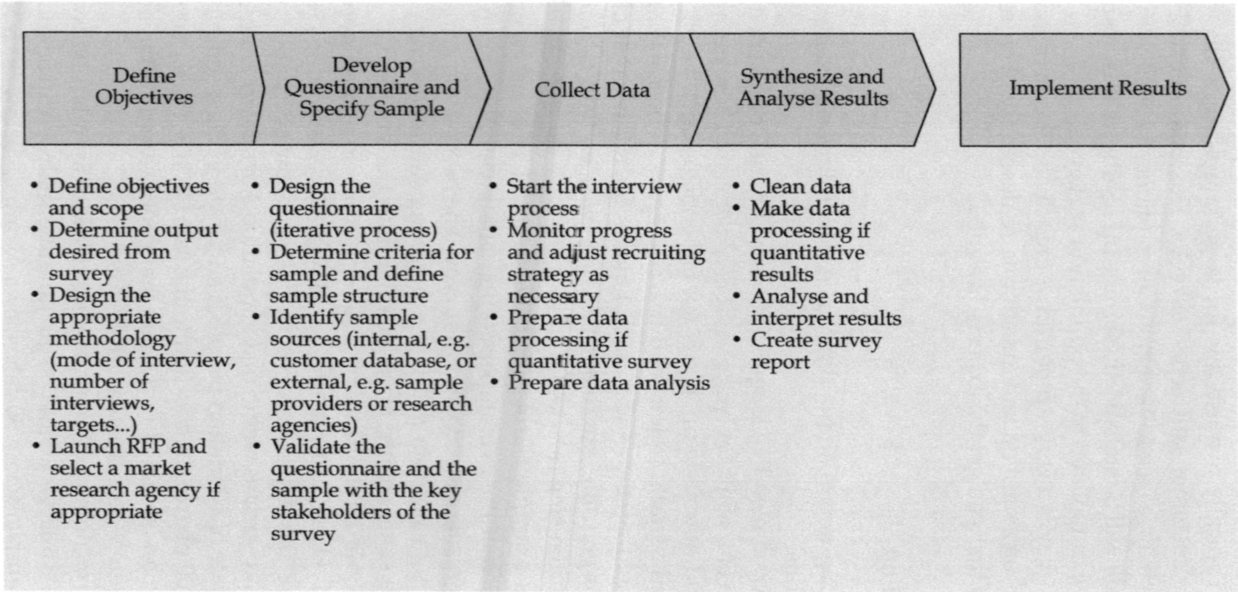

Define Objectives	Develop Questionnaire and Specify Sample	Collect Data	Synthesize and Analyse Results	Implement Results
• Define objectives and scope • Determine output desired from survey • Design the appropriate methodology (mode of interview, number of interviews, targets...) • Launch RFP and select a market research agency if appropriate	• Design the questionnaire (iterative process) • Determine criteria for sample and define sample structure • Identify sample sources (internal, e.g. customer database, or external, e.g. sample providers or research agencies) • Validate the questionnaire and the sample with the key stakeholders of the survey	• Start the interview process • Monitor progress and adjust recruiting strategy as necessary • Prepare data processing if quantitative survey • Prepare data analysis	• Clean data • Make data processing if quantitative results • Analyse and interpret results • Create survey report	

Source: Developed by Charlotte Raut, Accenture Research, Paris.

Assuming you have the following composition of your eco-system, you could come up with the samples sizes represented in Table 6.4.

TABLE 6.4
Sampling

Population and Size	Illustrative Sample Size
5,000 employees	1,000
30 management trustees	6
100 donors	30
200 volunteers	50
5 ministries (public health, inner security, finance, social affairs, general administration)	25 (5 per ministry)
20 politicians	4
2 newspapers	2–4 (1–2 per newspaper)

Source: Compiled by the authors.

Representativity of the sample is also critical to guarantee meaningful and relevant results that you can extrapolate to a larger population. You need to ensure that all the major groups in your population are adequately represented. The representativity of the sample is monitored via quotas (that is, target numbers of interviews with sub-groups) that are defined on the basis of the actual structure of the population analysed. For example, if you want to make an opinion poll of the general population of a country, you need to structure your sample in a way that it makes it completely comparable to the general population according to some key components: typical criteria used for sampling, when it deals with large consumer surveys, are gender, age, professional occupations and regions.

Again, the important rule in sampling is not how many poll respondents are selected but, instead, how they are selected. A reliable sample selects poll respondents randomly or in a manner that insures that everyone in the area being surveyed has a known chance of being selected.

Questionnaire Design

As to the questionnaire design: there are a number of rules to consider before one starts compiling it. First of all, you need to customize your questionnaire (content, length, phrasing of the questions) to the approach (qualitative versus quantitative), methodology (face to face, phone, web, mail) and respondents' profiles (targeted professional versus consumers).

Apart from that, arrange your questions in the following way:

1. Go from general to particular.
2. Go from easy to difficult.
3. Go from factual to abstract.
4. Do not start with demographic and personal questions unless you need it to filer your target group, for example, people over 60 years.

You might again apply the MECE principle you learned about earlier, which requires that all issues listed are mutually exclusive and collectively exhaustive (MECE). In other words you do not ask anything twice and you include all relevant questions.

Another key success factor of a questionnaire is to always ask questions in the most neutral way in order to not influence responses.

POCA would like to understand two things better to tailor their community services and secure funding to provide the same:

- What are the specific needs of children with HIV/AIDS?
- What are the expectations of decision makers which would make them work with POCA?

POCA decides to combine a qualitative and a quantitative survey to answer both questions. They send a standardized questionnaire in the local language to parents, hospitals, community leads as well as other NGOs to get a better and consolidated view about children's needs. Based on the knowledge that they have gained from this first exercise they reach out to decision-makers in the public sector to better understand their drivers. As they have just conducted the survey early on, they can position themselves as experts with a current and fresh view on the specific issue.

INP+ (Indian Network for People living with HIV/AIDS) has used survey research intensively to formulate their strategy and provide evidence for their cause.

BEST PRACTICE CASE STUDY: INP+
(SERVING THE COMMUNITY SINCE 1997)

Indian Network for People living with HIV/AIDS (INP+), an 11-year-old national-level community-based organization is situated in Chennai in the south Indian state of Tamil Nadu. This Community Based Organization (CBO) exists purely for:

1. **PLHA Mobilization**
   Work towards mobilization for improved preventive care and enhanced quality of life of People Living with HIV/AIDS (PLHA) communities through systematic and continuous development of the networks at various levels — state, district and taluka levels.
2. **Human Rights**
   Campaigning for the elimination of discrimination and protection of the human rights of PLHA, particularly marginalized groups.
3. **Greater Involvement of People living with HIV/AIDS (GIPA)**
   Implementing and promoting GIPA and for the empowerment of PLHA with a view to creating an impact an existing programmes and policies.
4. **Access to Information and Services**
   Ensuring access to high quality information and services for positive prevention, positive living and continuation of care and treatment.
5. **Emerging Needs of PLHA**
   Responding to emerging needs of the PLHA community, including sustainable options for livelihood and social security.
6. **Positive Prevention**
   Assisting PLHA to adopt safe sexual practices as well as educating them on the use of safe injections. This helps not only in the prevention of transmission of infections to other people but also helps to protect the health of PLHA and their respective partners.

7. **Sustainable Organization**
   INP+ services are outcome focused, professionally managed, in partnership, evidence-based and sustainable.
8. **Promotion and Advocacy of all Drug and Vaccine Trials**
   Make sure that these are ethical, clearly explained, strictly monitored and that trial participants are fully insured against negative drug effects, through participatory involvement. And also to promote, through advocacy efforts, a research atmosphere, not only in medical research, but also in different fields that will benefit PLHA.

Mission and Core Component

To improve the quality of life of people living with HIV in India and provide a sense of belonging to PLHA and their families for full and active participation in the society and also to reduce further HIV transmission. The organization has tuned all its activities towards three core components — advocacy, network building and service delivery.

Advocacy

The CBO aims at addressing issues of the community members like access to treatment, access to information, human rights, GIPA, social acceptance of PLHA, an end to the stigma and discrimination and creating opportunities of networking for PLHA. Over the decade, INP+ in its chronicle has had significant success in advocacy for treatment access — ART and second line, or even promoting the concept of positive prevention.

Network Building

This component aims at the formation and strengthening of networks at state, district and taluka levels. Currently INP+ has 22 state-level networks and 221 district-level networks with a service membership crossing 114,000 across the country. It also aims to provide technical assistance to networks in capacity building at state and district levels on various subjects like programme management, service delivery, leadership and governance.

The State Level Networks (SLN) affiliated to INP+ are the face and voice of people living with HIV/AIDS across the states in India. Developing good links and a referral system with the State AIDS Control Societies, other stakeholders and partners working in the field of HIV/AIDS alongside involving other marginalized communities are the key activities taken up by them. They also provide services such as counselling, and information on positive living and life after infection to people leaving with AIDS (PLWHA). They also form and mentor District Level Networks (DLNs) and Taluka Level Networks (TLNs).

The DLNs are the base of the SLNs acting as the entry and service delivery points to PLWHA and other marginalized communities. To these people, DLNs provide direct services such as counselling, organizing and conducting community-level support group meetings, developing links with the local NGOs, distributing nutritional supplements, and so on.

All groups work completely independently. Nevertheless, should assistance be needed, the national-level network provides support in the form of expertise and technical assistance to the state level and the state level then provides the same support to the district level.

Service Delivery

INP+ has the credit of developing unique models of care and support services such as Drop-in-Centres (DIC), Life Focus Centres (LFC), Family Counselling Centres (FCC), Positive Living Centres (PLC), Treatment Counselling Centres (TCC), and so on, to community members, irrespective of age and gender.

The Family Counselling Centre was established in February 2004. Approximately 900 people per month make use of this service. The centre has become a one-stop shop for psychological counselling and medical care for people living with HIV/AIDS as well as their family members. The centre is based on a public–private partnership with the Government Hospital for Thoracic Medicine (GHTM), Tambaram. Six counsellors from INP+ and eight counsellors from GHTM work jointly at the centre. The Family Counselling Centre is supported by the Centres for Disease Control and Prevention

(CDC) of the Global AIDS Program (GAP), USA, and provides several services crucial to the health-care and support of people living with HIV/AIDS.

Funding

Main Sponsors/Donors

The organization relies upon on a broad ecosystem to enlarge its portfolio of services, including technical and financial support management, capacity building, as well as treatment and care. To enumerate a few:

1. National AIDS Control Organization
2. United States Agency for International Development
3. Family Health International
4. Bill & Melinda Gates Foundation
5. Centres for Disease Control and Prevention
6. United Nations Development Programme
7. Joint United Nations Programme on HIV/AIDS

Individuals, groups or organizations can make donations to support INP+ and its projects related to children and affected families, although individual donors only contribute $200 to $400 (about 10,000–20,000 INR) per year.

Other Key Strategies of INP+

Research

Research plays an important role in providing evidence for initiating policy change. Research reports are available on the website. The organization actually started using survey research to provide evidence for initiating policy change. INP+ initiated a project to document the needs of PLWHA in four cities of India, namely Bangalore, New Delhi, Mumbai and Imphal at end of the 1990s. In-depth interviews and focus group discussions were conducted with men and women living with HIV in these cities. Based on the findings of the study, a five-day strategy planning meeting was organized to formulate a strategy plan for the INP+ to address the needs of PLWHA. This draft workplan was presented to the donors and supporters in a meeting along with the findings of the study to disseminate the findings, involve the donors in PLWHA issues and to raise the profile of the organization.

A recent example is the 114 page research report, *Missing the Target: Improving AIDS Drug Access and Advancing Health Care for All* (December 2007) written by members of several NGOs throughout the world and which includes specific information about the situation in India by an IPN+ official. In general, reports focus on hot topics such as the inadequacy of drug provision or violent behaviour against homosexuals within countries where a large number of citizens suffer from HIV/AIDS. Moreover, the INP+ website provides the CBO's annual report.

Main External Communication Channels

INP+ predominantly engages in advocacy and directly addresses several institutions which are in charge of its area of focus at all policy levels in an attempt to initiate policy change. The main strategy of the INP+ is to lobby and put pressure on policy-makers, mainly by collecting evidence at the grassroots level.

INP+ strives to train people to advocate the issue of AIDS at the district, state and national levels. These people are educated, trained and empowered by INP+ and have been recognized as Positive Speakers. Through them, INP+ can participate in a larger number of workshops, forums and meetings at the different policy levels. Thus these Positive Speakers (combined with the enthusiasm of 'the power and the spirit' that comes from the grass roots, that is, the district-level networks) are the most important communication channels for INP+.

The key strategy intended by the organization to generate optimum awareness through outreach is utilizing extensive mass media communication. Other communication channels include workshops, one-to-one or group meetings with politicians, press releases or media presence in general (newspaper and television), emails, posters, pamphlets, research reports, events and 'positive speaking' through visits to schools and colleges. INP+ seeks to improve and leverage the integration of its different communication channels but currently lacks the necessary resources to do so. The NGO also has access to sufficient capabilities to further exploit the opportunities of online communication.

Main Internal Communication Channels

On a quarterly basis, the organization has regular board meetings and decisions are communicated via email or letters to the staff. There are staff members dedicated to the documentation and communication among district, state and national levels with the main communication channels being write-ups of discussions, minutes of meetings and reports, including updates and information, all of which is then sent to all staff and board members.

Campaigns

The NGO not only initiates issue-based campaigns, but also engages in permanent campaigning to raise awareness and educate the people. However, mainly due to the lack of resources the focus falls on issue-based campaigning. One of the most successful ways of campaigning is petitioning or public protest in the form of sit-ins in front of institutional buildings. In addition it conducts rallies and internet campaigning through their website.

One performance indicator for the evaluation of the campaign's is people's change in reaction to the issue. Another performance indicator is an actual policy change. 'If the policy changes, then it is a success' (K. K. Abraham, President of INP+ in a personal interview with Sarah Bastgen, February 2008, Chennai).

The overall aim of INP+ organizing campaigns is to turn the attention of the policy-makers towards the rights and issues of PLWHA and most of the efforts taken to this day have yielded positive responses such as a concession for transportation costs to PLWHA, the distribution of medicine in GHTM, Tambaram and many more such actions. Although the result of the campaigns conducted cannot be measured in percentages, the evidence of success can be gauged by the changes in policy.

Contact

Indian Network for People living with HIV/AIDS (INP+)
Flat No 6, Kasha Towers
No 93 (New No 121), South West Bag Road
T. Nagar
Chennai – 600 017
Phone: + 91 44 2432 9580/81
Fax: + 91 44 2432 9582
Email: inp@inpplus.net; inpplus@vsnl.com; inpplus@eth.net
Website: http://www.inpplus.net

Chapter Seven

Strategy

Imagination is more important than knowledge.

Albert Einstein

THIS SECTION provides the tools necessary to define who one wants to be in the future. It is necessary to define your overall strategy which is the prerequisite to defining your organizational goals and positioning.

Questions answered are:

1. What do I want to achieve?
2. How do I get there?
3. How can I strategically differentiate?
4. How do I take the organization along?

STRATEGIC INTENT

*We sometimes from dreams pick up some
hint worth improving by ... reflection.*

Thomas Jefferson

The term 'Strategic Intent' was introduced by Gary Hamel and C. K. Prahalad in an article with the same name published in *Harvard Business Review* in 1989 (Hamel and Prahalad 1989). In this article, written in light of increasing perception of Japanese competition, the authors explain that western companies have wasted too much time and energy replicating the cost and quality advantages their global competitors have already experienced. Other than a static approach to competitive positioning by analyzing what is happening in the market and copying it, it starts with something different and ambitious. It refers to the corporate goals that are designed to inspire a company and its employees, ideally over a long period of time. It is by far more than a 'buzzword expression': it is the basis of an organization's identity. One famous example is Coca Cola's claim to be within 'an arm's reach of every consumer in the world'.

The strategic intent is a powerful and well-thought through statement of where one wants to be at a given time. To return to the example of our organization, the intent could be formulated as follows:
'POCA is India's heart and home for children with HIV/AIDS.'
   While formulating its strategic intent to define where an organization wants to be, it will be prerequisite to take one's people along by:

1. Boldly addressing the issue of children with HIV/AIDS in India.
2. Working with local communities to improve prevention of HIV/AIDS.
3. Working with decision makers and opinion makers to improve educational and health infrastructure for infected children.
4. Ensuring that health related policies on the state and national levels address the specific needs of this particular group which is appropriate and relevant.

MISSION/VISION STATEMENT

Vision is the art of seeing something invisible.

Jonathan Swift

A vision statement is the summary of where an organization wants to be in an ideal world. It should contain the purpose, strategy, values and necessary behaviour to follow.

The vision statement is often lumped together with a mission statement and tackles the question why we are in business and how things are done.

The mission of our organization can be developed as follows:

1. Our organization addresses one of the most pressing problems of our time and wants to make a difference in India (Purpose: why are we doing what we are doing).
2. We want to become the leading organization providing health and social services to children suffering from HIV (Strategy: what we want to do and how we are relatively positioned).
3. We believe in equal rights and the politics of inclusion (Set of values: beliefs providing the fundamentals for interaction with employees, stakeholders and customers).
4. We are committed to providing access to fairness, medical treatment and showing respect for everyone (Behaviours: how we do things — our most important standards).

DIFFERENTIATION

It is the difference of opinions that makes horse races.

Mark Twain

Differentiation is one of the key principles of corporate strategy. The objective is to maintain a competitive differentiation so as to attract more donors and supporters than other organizations in the same policy field. Based on the analysis of the market and competition, we are now well positioned to define a Unique Selling Proposition (USP). This is far more than an intellectual exercise — this is the sentence one should come up when are sharing the elevator for 45 seconds with the person one has wanted as a supporter for years. Very often, you have only one opportunity to get a person's attention and the more clearly you have thought about who you are in the market, the more likely you will be able to raise interest. In other words, what is it what differentiates you from other organizations in your specific field?

Some examples for POCA could be:

1. You are embedded in and work with the community.
2. You have a holistic approach, working in prevention as well as providing medical services to infected children.
3. You have a strong partner network, enriching your portfolio of services as well as increasing your knowledge base.
4. You integrate infected children so that they can define their needs through a 'positive kids parliament', thereby making them agents of change.
5. You launch a specific conference/workshop series, something which is considered key in presenting and distributing knowledge on kids with HIV/AIDS.

Room to Read, an NGO operating in the policy field of education can be considered a best practice in differentiation. On a global scale, there are many successful organizations that have been operating in the policy field for years. However, Room to Read has successfully differentiated itself and has made a real impact on children in Asia and Africa.

BEST PRACTICE CASE STUDY: ROOM TO READ

Vision/Mission

Room to Read partners with local communities throughout the developing world to provide quality educational opportunities to disadvantaged children. They seek to intervene early in the lives of children in the belief that education empowers people to improve socio-economic conditions of their families, communities, countries and future generations. Through the opportunities that only education can provide, we strive to break the cycle of poverty, one child at a time.

Approach

Room to Read has developed a strategic, long-term, and holistic approach to help children in the developing world to gain access to education and knowledge. This approach includes five core programs:

1. School Room – it partners with villages to build new schools, replace dilapidated structures, or expand schools to alleviate overcrowded classrooms.
2. Reading Room – it establishes bilingual libraries and fills them local language and English language children's books, posters, maps, and games that engage children in literacy.
3. Local Language Publishing – it works with local writers and illustrators to create and publish high-quality local language children's books to distribute to its own libraries and throughout the organization's networks.
4. Computer Room – it establishes computer labs to provide students with skills such as technology literacy and global awareness.
5. Room to Grow Girls' Scholarship – it also funds long-term girls' scholarships for underprivileged girls to ensure their ability to complete secondary school.

Room to Read currently operates in eight countries — six in Asia (Cambodia, India, Laos, Nepal, Sri Lanka, and Vietnam) and two in Africa (South Africa and Zambia), with plans to expand throughout Asia, Africa and Latin America in the years to come to better meet the needs of children throughout the developing world.

In order to increase its impact and long-term sustainability with every investment, Room to Read requests community involvement and co-investment through a 'challenge grant' model. Villages often raise a significant portion of the overall expenditure in the form of dedicated space, labour, materials and (or) small amounts of cash. These 'challenge grants' act as catalysts for community building while simultaneously maximizing the local participation and expertise brought to Room to Read's programmes. The organization hires local staff that has a vested interest in their nation's educational progress and then empowers them to make key programme decisions within their own country. Room to Read believes that because local staff are familiar with the language, conditions, customs and culture, they are best equipped to seek out the most effective solutions to address educational needs in their community.

Background

Room to Read was founded in 2000 by John Wood, a former Microsoft executive. He launched the organization following a trek through Nepal, which inspired him to help bring educational resources to the world's poorest communities. Driven to make a difference, he left Microsoft and built a global team to work with local communities to implement sustainable solutions to their educational needs. Table 7.1 provides a brief chronology of the history of Room to Read.

Room to Read is a dynamic, results-focused organization. Since its inception in 2000, it has had an impact on the lives of more than 1.7 million children by:

1. constructing 442 schools; and
2. establishing over 5,100 libraries.

TABLE 7. 1
Room to Read—History

Year	Details
1999	In late 1999, John Wood quit his executive position with Microsoft to start Room to Read.
2000	Room to Read launched its School Room and Reading Room Programmes.
2001	In the summer of 2001, Erin Ganju joined the team as Chief Operating Officer and was instrumental in its expansion into Vietnam. They expanded Room to Read's geographic and programmatic presence and launched the Girls' Scholarship Program.
2002	In response to growing demand for its programmes, Room to Read expanded into Cambodia.
2003	In 2003 Room to Read expanded into India. It began publishing local language children's books, to supplement the donated English language books used to stock its libraries.
2004	Room to Read celebrated one of its first major milestones on April 29th when it opened its 1,000th library in Siem Reap, Cambodia. Later that year, just days after the December 24th Asian tsunami devastated thousands of villages; it made the bold decision to launch operations in Sri Lanka in order to rebuild schools there.
2005	In addition to expanding into Sri Lanka in 2005, Room to Read began working in Laos, marking its 5th and 6th Asian countries of operation. On 2 September, it opened its 2,000th library, once again in Cambodia, less than 18 months after its 1,000th library ceremony. Room to Read ended 2005 with another big milestone, the donation of the one millionth books.
2006	Room to Read expanded its work into a new continent, Africa, by launching programmes in South Africa in April. In December, it celebrated the one millionth child to benefit from its work.
2007	In February 2007 Room to Read established a presence in a second African country by launching programs in Zambia. In addition, it established its 5,000th library in Nepal.

Source: Room to Read. 2008.

3. donating over 2.2 million English language children's books;
4. publishing 226 new local language children's titles in 19 languages, representing over two million books;
5. funding over 4,000 long-term girls' scholarships; and
6. establishing 155 computer and language labs.

By the end of 2010, Room to Read programs will have reached over 5 million children worldwide.

Room to Read has been widely recognized for its contribution to the field of social entrepreneurship. The organization's founder, John Wood, was selected as one of *TIME* magazine's 'Asian Heroes' in 2004 — the only non-Asian ever to win this honour. He was also awarded the Skoll Award for Social Entrepreneurship in 2006. Finally, Room to Read has received the Fast Company/Monitor Group 'Social Capitalist' award for the last five years — one of only 10 non-profits to have received this honour every year since the award was created.

Organizational Structure/Way of Decision Making

Room to Read is headed by a Chief Executive Officer (CEO) and an 11-person board of trustees. Additionally, Room to Read also has a nine-person advisory board that provides counsel on operational issues. The board of trustees meets quarterly and the advisory board meets bi-annually, with conference calls organized between meetings as needed.

Room to Read has approximately 250 paid employees worldwide.

Members and Volunteers

Room to Read does not have individual members, but it does have a large network of volunteers organized geographically into local 'chapters'. In 2008 Room to Read's volunteer network grew to 35 worldwide 'chapters', with more than 3,000 volunteers networking, planning events and raising awareness within their communities about Room to Read. Through the local 'chapter' structure, these volunteers raised a significant portion of Room to Read's operating budget for 2007.

Funding

The budget for 2008 is US$26 million and includes cash and gifts-in-kind (through its English language book donation program). The majority of Room to Read's funding originates from individual donations. It has over 25,000 individual donors, primarily in the US, but also in other major cities around the globe. The remainder of Room to Read's funding comes from foundations and corporate giving programmes.

Table 7.2 lists the organization's top foundation and corporate donors.

TABLE 7. 2
Historicaly Top 10 Corporate and Foundation Donors

Rank	Constituent Name	Amount Given (US$)
1.	Skoll Foundation	1,519,000
2.	Accenture Foundation	1,314,970
3.	Goldman Sachs Foundation	777, 825
4.	Four Acre Trust	582,822
5.	Microsoft	546,511
6.	Qualcomm	529,895
7.	The Michael and Susan Dell Foundation	437,500
8.	Credit Suisse Group Foundation	406,950
9.	Tudor Investment Corporation	359,444
10.	Charities Aid Foundation	316,286

Source: Room to Read. 2008.
Note: The list above does not include gifts-in-kind and covers donations received from 1 January 2000 through 11 June 2008.

Networking

Room to Read, as an organization, networks with a variety of local, regional and international NGOs with the goal of creating synergies to improve its programs, as well as building the field for international education. They formally partner with a variety of NGOs at the local level, as described below in the section on 'Partnerships with other NGOs'. They also encourage their network of over 3,000 'chapter' volunteers to collaborate with individuals, corporations, foundations and schools in their communities to raise visibility and funding for Room to Read.

Governance

Room to Read has national offices in all eight countries in which it currently operates. It also has a number of provincial offices in most of these countries. Furthermore, Room to Read has an Asia regional office in Delhi, India, which oversees all Asia country offices, and it is in the process of establishing a Southern Africa regional office in Pretoria, South Africa. The global office staff in San Francisco communicates with country and regional staff to gather information about programmes and operations and to share relevant information from the US headquarters. Collaboration among the country, regional and global offices is an important part of the organization's operational structure.

Partnership with other NGOs

Room to Read collaborates with a number of local NGOs in its eight countries of operation that similarly focus on education and development. The organization partners with these local NGOs to create synergies; in some countries the partnership is a legal pre-requisite for Room to Read to operate. The partnerships with local NGOs include both project-specific and long-term collaborations, depending on the circumstances and requirements of the project. Room to Read does not have formal partnerships with any regional or international NGOs.

Communication Strategies

Main External Communication Channels and Strategies

Room to Read uses a variety of strategies to communicate with its constituents. The organization has an active presence in top domestic and international media outlets across the globe. Many of the articles have focused on the founder, John Wood, and the story of his life as a social entrepreneur. In 2006 he published a biography entitled *Leaving Microsoft to Change the World: An Entrepreneur's Odyssey to Educate the World's Children*, which has become a successful element of the organization's marketing approach. Increasingly, media focus is shifting from the founder to the global organization and its efforts in the field of international education. An example of this is the PBS *FRONTLINE/World* documentary entitled 'Nepal: A Girl's Life', which examines Room to Read's work at ground-level in Nepal from the perspective of a girl benefiting from the scholarship programme.

From a traditional marketing and public relations standpoint, Room to Read's communication approach includes media outlets, television, print media (newspapers, magazines), online channels (email and website) and collateral (printed) materials. The organization's main communication channels include the website, email (targeted to an active group of donors), speeches and public appearances by the CEO, a quarterly newsletter (distributed by email), and periodic fundraising events organized by its volunteer 'chapters'. Furthermore, Room to Read organizes an annual conference of its 'chapter' leadership, bringing together the most active members of the volunteer network to share best practices and build networks for mutual learning and support. To communicate with its constituents within the countries of operation, local staff relies on face-to-face meetings, email, telephone and fax.

Research on Communication

Room to Read already has components of a strategic communications plan already in place, including a public relations strategy, a marketing and a branding strategy. To strengthen its communication work, it is currently working with a consulting company to assist with market research and benchmarking. In addition, every three to five years Room to Read engages in an organization-wide strategic planning process to determine future directions. As part of this process, it researches and considers key internal and external factors in updating the communication plan for the organization.

Main Internal Communication Channels and Strategies

Internally, Room to Read relies primarily on email to communicate with its staff at the global office in San Francisco; the Asia regional office in Delhi and all the country and provincial offices in Asia (Cambodia, India, Laos, Nepal, Sri Lanka and Vietnam) and Africa (South Africa and Zambia). Within each office, the staff also communicates through regular face-to-face meetings, individual team meetings and all-staff meetings. On a regular basis, Room to Read also organizes conferences which bring together groups of employees working on similar topics. For example, it has an annual meeting of country directors, as well as annual or bi-annual meetings of programme staff.

To ensure the flow of communication, Room to Read shares a wide variety of reports and documents through the organization's internal public documents drive, the internal donor database (called Raiser's Edge), and through the newly implemented Global Systems Database, which provides real-time data about the organization's programmes originating directly from field offices. The marketing and public relations department also has a newly created public relations database for tracking contacts and media coverage. Additionally, to measure marketing (public relations) reach, Room to Read is beginning to utilize Google docs, Google alerts and Google analytics.

Advertising/Marketing

Room to Read's website is currently the organization's most important marketing (public relations) tool, although it also uses printed materials, including an annual report, a tri-fold brochure and an annual 'yearbook' on the girls' scholarship programme. In addition, Room to Read is negotiating a contract for a new email programme, from which it can disseminate newsletters and breaking news items to its network of stakeholders.

Stakeholders

Room to Read has two key sets of stakeholders: the children that benefit from its programmes and its donors. Donors include individuals, foundations, corporations, schools and 'chapter' leaders.

Contact

Room to Read
111 Sutter Street
16th floor
San Francisco, CA 94104
United States
(415)561-3331 (Phone)
(415)561-0580 (Fax)
Website: http://www.roomtoread.org/

STRATEGY FORMULATION

Formulating a strategy helps to assess an organizations current status and articulates where it wants to be. In the process of formulating this, you basically decide what procedure to follow. Based on the analysis and thinking which has been done, one is now able to bring it all together.

> A summary of our strategy going forward in order to become the leading NGO in this policy field would be:
> Situation Analysis:
>
> 1. Patchy infrastructure to support the needs of children with HIV/AIDS. There are organizations addressing HIV/AIDS and others focusing on children and health, but no organization looks at the combined problem.
> 2. Lots of activity of international organizations and opportunity to work with them.
> 3. However, this topic is still taboo in India, and lots of effort is required to increase awareness and garner public support from key stakeholders.

Ideally, all the analysis that has been done should be in the strategy document. This point is not only obviously convenient as everything is in one place, but it can also be used as a reference document with stakeholders. Taking stakeholders along is crucial. A strategy that people do not buy into is absolutely useless and becomes nothing but a piece of paper.

STRATEGY IMPLEMENTATION

There is nothing wrong with change, if it is in the right direction.

Winston Churchill

After formulating the strategy, implementation begins, this is 95 per cent of the work! Right at the beginning of your strategy process it is required to take the whole organization into the change management journey. Key members of the strategy team act as 'change ambassadors'. The task now is to modify organizational structures, processes and culture to construct the innovative way to position the organization in the market. Culture is the most challenging part. It is thus essential that milestones are clearly set during that journey. One option that can be used to track this is to create a scorecard with key performance indicators. One might consider doing this on a monthly basis, for example. Such a scorecard provides a good tool for reporting back to key stakeholders.

ORGANIZATIONAL ALIGNMENT

Take my assets – but leave me my organization and in five years I'll have it all back.

Alfred M. Sloan

No job will be done without people supporting it. Particularly in a change situation (and there are frankly no 'business as usual' times anymore), motivated employees who believe that the organization is striving for the right objectives are a prerequisite for success. Thus, the top of the agenda should be to take the people along. Quite often, changes make people feel uncomfortable, especially if they feel they do not understand what is going on and what the implication for their role and day-to-day job will be. As such, there are three things which need to be done: communicate, communicate and communicate. It doesn't help though if everything is thrown at everyone at once.

As some key people have already been included into the governing process, it will also equip them with knowledge about the process. They will not only help you during your strategy process, they will also serve as ambassadors of change in the organizations further afield. After achieving the milestones you have defined in your work plan, communication to the wider group is recommended. As mentioned, there are three main areas which require your attention:

1. Structure: it is necessary to take a close look at the way one's organization is structured. So, following the principle 'structure follows strategy', one can start to make one's organization slimmer, more flexible and more directed towards the interest of the people supported. In order to fully implement this and to get people to buy into this, allow this organizational structure to persist for at least two years.

2. Processes: How does this new structure impact all the support functions? What HR processes does one need? How does one's tailor marketing or one's facilities run? At this point in time, it is of paramount importance to take a close look at the professional development processes, rewards and recognition, as well as adopt measures to motivate employees. Expressing an appreciation for employees will make a huge difference to the atmosphere.

3. Culture: Whereas the structure can be changed quickly, followed by the processes, the alteration of the cultural aspects will take its time. The most important thing is that the leadership lives and breathes the new culture both in communication and practices. A very important basis for this is the institutionalization of a learning culture, facing up to the fact that this is a joint journey based on a shared vision. In order to achieve this, one needs to manage the organizational change thoughtfully in a tailored, change management process.

Political Communication

*The most important thing in communication
is hearing what isn't said.*

Peter Drucker

IN THIS chapter, strategic tools are introduced to generate insights
to communicate the issue that the NGO addresses. A key focus
will be on the 'how' of communicating findings. Each of the tools
introduced will be illustrated by a case study from relevant policy
fields. Areas in focus are human rights, environment, women and
gender issues, public health, child rights and European issues.
  Questions answered are:

1. Who are my most important stakeholders? The tool introduced here is stakeholder analysis.
2. Where can I address the issue? The tool introduced here is
   power mapping.
3. How can I address the issue? The tool here is strategic communication planning.

STAKEHOLDER ANALYSIS

All for one, one for all.

Alexandre Dumas, *The Three Musketeers*

Formulating a strategy in isolation from those who have to drive
it or will be impacted by it in one way or another will not be

successful. Profit and non-profit organizations likewise have to consider the world around them when formulating their objectives or gaining support. Engaging with stakeholders is the *sine qua non* for motivating their commitment and support. Understanding one's stakeholders can be useful for a number of purposes. It can be geared towards an understanding for which interests need to be taken into account when campaigning for a policy change or to get a view on whom to target in order to increase donations.

Stakeholders or 'interested parties' can be grouped into categories as shown in Table 8.1.

TABLE 8.1
Stakeholder Groups

Private Sector Stakeholders	*Public Sector Stakeholders*	*Civil Society Stakeholders*
• Corporation and businesses	• Ministers and advisors (executive)	• Media
• Business associations	• Civil servants and departments (bureaucracy)	• Churches/religions
• Professional bodies	• Elected representatives (legislature)	• Schools and Universities
	• Courts (judiciary)	• Social movements and advocacy groups
• Individual business leader	• Political parties	• Trade unions
• Financial institutions	• Local government/councils	• National NGOs
	• Military	• International NGOs
	• Quangos and commissions	
	• International bodies (World Bank, UN)	

Source: Hovland, I. and D. Start. 2004. *Tools for Policy Impact: A Handbook for Researchers*. London: Overseas Development Institute.

Obviously the first step, to come up with the overall objective, is a question of why the stakeholder analysis should be done at all. How can this help to address the question of what the problem is to be solved? In the case of our NGO, we would obviously use the analysis to understand better how to optimize support in our ecosystem to ensure financial sustainability. To do that, we first need to list all our stakeholders based on the categories mentioned above. You might also like to use indicators to show particular and individual strengths — indicators such as 1, 2, 3, and so on.

After you have compiled the list, group the people into the categories as shown in Table 8.2.

TABLE 8.2
Stakeholder Analysis Worksheet

Name/Organization	Relationship to NGO	Interest in NGO	Decision Maker	Access to Resources

Source: Developed by the authors.

This can be done in either of two ways: by either working on this with the organization or by creating a questionnaire for direct interaction with one's stakeholders. The latter approach is far more time consuming, but might be useful for an NGO which depends to a large extent on its respective support system. Also, it might help understand what is driving them to either support or not support you. In business, the term 'buyer values' is used to describe this. It is crucial to the process of positioning an organization so as to understand the value and belief system of potential supporters.

POWER MAPPING

A power map will help to address the right people in an appropriate manner and to understand how strong their influence is to support the case. Furthermore, one needs to have a clear understanding of who the opponents are and whom one needs to influence to take them along. A power map helps in doing that (see Figure 8.1).

It is important to distinguish between approvers, decision makers and opinion makers and rate their influence on your key issues from strong to weak.

After you have this finalized, you may also group your stakeholders into categories of support as shown in Table 8.3.

TABLE 8.3
Mapping Stakeholders

	Moderate		Moderate	
Strong Supporter	Supporter	Neutral	Opponent	Opponent

Source: Developed by the authors.

FIGURE 8.1
Sample Power Map

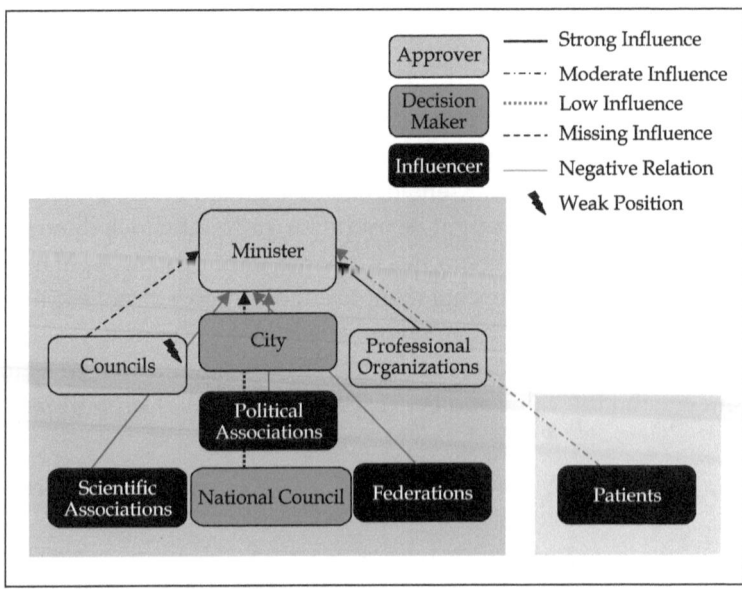

Source: Developed by the authors.

First you quantify based on your table:

1. How many supporters do you have?
2. Who are the most important stakeholders?
3. Why specific stakeholders support or oppose you? (Interest analysis).
4. Which stakeholders might form alliances to your benefit?

5. How many opponents do you have?
6. Who are the most important opponents?
7. Which opponents might form alliances to your disadvantage?
8. Who are the neutral stakeholders, what is their importance and what interests do they have?

The approach of the stakeholder analysis helps you structure and systematically understand the ecosystem. Now you can start to work more intensively with your supporters, allowing them to form alliances. You can also start to turn your opponents into supporters.

POCA has done this exercise and has got a good understanding of who would support their cause and more importantly, who would be in the position to make decisions in their interest. Their key objective is to link the issue of HIV/AIDS and health policies meeting the needs of children.

Butterflies is an example of best practice in attracting and managing stakeholders. Through this approach, they have created a broad network and synergies for their cause.

Best Practice Case Study: Butterflies

Vision/Mission

Butterflies believes in the right of every child to have a full-fledged childhood where she or he has the right to protection, respect, opportunities and participation in his or her growth and development. Their vision is, 'A world where every child is free to be a child and has hope for the future.' The main objective of Butterflies is to apply these rights to runaways, homeless kids and working children. The organization wants to empower street children and working children through capacity building, skills and knowledge so as to protect their rights and to develop them into respectable citizens leading a life which is meaningful to them.

Approach

Butterflies is committed to a non-institutional approach and promotes children's democratic participation in decision making, planning, monitoring and evaluation as a crucial part of its programme. Thus Butterflies refuses the institutional approach of putting children in separate homes. On the contrary, the organization tries to reintegrate the children to their families. If this is not an option because it is a dysfunctional family or because the child would have to face extreme poverty which would threaten his or her physical or psychological well-being, Butterflies offers tailored services to empower children to strive for a meaningful life with dignity. Through their approach, the organization has established so-called 'contact points' to meet the children where they are rather than have them come to their institution. The locations could be anywhere: bus stops, railway stations, market places, parks, or other places where the children work or live. This is where the NGO tries to contact and build rapport with the children to motivate them to join their education programmes, thus gaining the knowledge and skills for breaking the poverty cycle. Butterflies is in contact with more than 2,000 street and working children on a regular basis through 12 contact points in Delhi. They also work with 6,000 children in tsunami affected villages of Andaman and Nicobar Islands. Butterflies' strategy aims to ensure that children actively participate in the decision-making process and this is done through their *Bal Sabha* (children's council meetings) and their own *Bal Mazdoor Union* (child workers union). Monthly *Bal Sabha* meetings are forums where they discuss all the issues which affect their lives, share their concerns and find collective solutions. Guided by the adult child rights facilitator and based on their needs and Butterflies' vision, the children also plan their future activities as part of the Butterflies programme. They thus learn the principles of democracy, that is, every person has a right to an opinion and freedom of expression and that a consensus must be reached to take a final decision; but they also learn that sometimes a compromise is needed. *Bal Sabha* is at the core of Butterflies' programme and is now a regular forum for children to share their concerns, and at the same time it also helps us to refine our programme interventions.

Butterflies strives to make the Convention on the Rights of the Child a reality, particularly for those children who are most vulnerable, neglected, abused and exploited. Basically, it is an organization that is committed to promoting solidarity among NGOs, government and all civil society organizations for addressing the well-being of all children.

Background

Since 1989, Butterflies has been a registered voluntary organization. The NGO's staff strength in Delhi is about 81. Butterflies is active in mainland India, the Andaman and Nicobar Islands and parts of South Asia.

Butterflies is led by the founding director and a core team of seven people as departmental heads of programmes and initiatives. In addition, the NGO has a board consisting of seven people, including the director, the administrator and the programme facilitators. The director is responsible for ensuring that decision making based on best judgment. Programme related decisions are made by the core group of senior staff, and policy decisions are made by the board in consultation with the director. Often staff suggestions on policy change and review or additions to existing policy are endorsed by the board. With regards to programme-related decisions, the children's council meeting has a crucial role. Meetings take place at every contact point on a monthly basis where all questions and issues are discussed and then acted upon in the fortnightly staff meeting and in the core group meetings.

Members and Volunteers

Apart from a few exceptions Butterflies does not work with volunteers, but has approximately five interns (tenure varies from two weeks up to one year). In most cases interns are students from colleges for social work, medical science or law. Depending on their expertise, interns are involved in all areas of the NGO's work and play a very important and crucial role in fundraising and creating awareness of the organization's work. Butterflies has no members who pay membership fees.

Most Important Stakeholder

Butterflies' most important stakeholders are primarily the children and their parents, although donors, employers, government, hospitals and medical services as well as the general community are also crucial to its work.

Funding

The budget for the entire Delhi-based programme is about US $1,500,000 (640,424,995 INR) per year. Major donors are international funding agencies, the Government of India, the Delhi State Government and the Municipal Corporation of Delhi.

Butterflies also receives support from corporate and individual donors. The official website has a brief description of options supporting Butterflies and its projects. According to the site, there are several ways to support Butterflies: one can sponsor, for example, the vocational training centre, the computer training project, the vocational training for future electricians or the community kitchen. Support is given either by donating a certain amount of money or by providing food or computer equipment. Another example is the option of 'payroll giving'. Each month an individual or group of employees can set an amount he or she wishes to donate on a monthly basis.

'Want to hear a butterfly giggle?' is another fund-raising campaign. By referring to the difficult circumstances in which these children live, Butterflies directly addresses potential donors: 'In our aspiration to reach out to more and more number of children we look towards YOU as it is your support and contribution that can make a difference to their lives and collectively all of us can make a difference in the lives of millions of children who need care and protection' (Interview with Butterflies, February 2008). Furthermore, Table 8.4 shows potential donors the amount of money that is needed to sponsor a certain project.

TABLE 8.4
Examples of Costs Associated with Support

Butterfly Project	Sponsorship Amount
Educate a child	INR 1,500/month ($37/month)
Sponsor a vocational training	INR 2,500/month ($61/month)
Support our sports and culture club	INR 250/month ($7/month)
Sponsor a brick for our crisis centre	INR 500/month ($13/month)

Source: http://www.butterflieschildrights.org/giggle.asp (Accessed in May 2008).

Main Sponsors and Donors

Basically Butterflies' main donors are a mix of government, corporations and NGOs from other countries: Misereor, Germany; Comic Relief, UK; Childhope, UK; the Ministry of Women and Child Development, Government of India; the Department of Education, Government of India; the Municipal Corporation of

Delhi; Atlantic Philanthropies, UK; Social Initiatives, Sweden; ICCO Netherlands; Railway Children, UK; the Hong Kong Shanghai Banking Corporation (HSBC), India.

Networks

Butterflies does not have any subsidiaries but two of its projects, the Children's Development Bank (http://www.childrens developmentbank.org/) and the children's newspaper, are now run by partnering NGOs and have gone to other parts of the country or abroad (Afghanistan, Nepal, etc.). Although the bank management board is set up by children and supported by a 'leading agency' in each country, namely an NGO, the 'key leading agency' is Butterflies. The aim of the Children's Development Bank (CDB) is to ensure that both street kids and working children have the opportunity to save their earnings in a way which gives them the possibility of using it wisely instead of squandering it quickly. In this way, the bank can even issue a little credit to children older than 15 to start small enterprises or improve themselves educationally. The 400 plus CDB account holders — mostly 'rag pickers' and street-children — own and run the bank from its headquarters at a night shelter for homeless children. Many of the children, some as young as 10 and 11, sell newspapers, boxes of tissues and other wares at traffic intersections. Some work on daily wages. Others collect waste and then sell it for recycling.

The *National Children's Times* (NCT) is a newspaper written, edited and published by street kids and working children between the ages of 9 and 14 on behalf of the National Child Journalist Forum and facilitated by Butterflies. This is the consequence of a constantly evolving movement which was initiated by the Child Workers Union in 1996. NCT is published once every two months in Hindi and English. Tearing down regional borders, the editorial team of the first small newspaper widened the project to address as many children as possible. It highlights various social issues concerning children that are otherwise neglected by the mainstream media. The main goal of the young authors is to provide information about topics which are usually not addressed by mainstream media although they urgently need attention.

Research

Research is an integral part of their programme:

1. It is directed towards strengthening the knowledge base on the issue of child protection, survival and development.
2. It develops evidence based advocacy strategies.
3. It guides and develops the Butterflies Programme through action research.
4. It advocates and initiates public discourse on issues relating to child rights, survival and development.
5. It functions as a resource centre on children for the government, voluntary development organizations, academic institutions, individuals, researchers and the public.

The Advocacy and Research Centre (ARC) is a unit of Butterflies that undertakes research and documentation to support not only advocacy but also facilitates action on issues of child rights. Realizing the importance of advocacy, research and documentation, ARC has been involved in doing relevant research in areas of child rights violations and child development. It is also responsible for the collection of relevant data on children as well as its documentation and analysis. On a regular basis, ARC brings out advocacy materials on child rights, including a series of comic books. Its mandate is that of specific evidence-based research, which will lead to action on cases of child rights violations. Sample reports are:

1. 'Plan of Action for Working Children in Delhi—To address the situation arising from the recent notification declaring a ban on employment of children in domestic work, eateries and *dabhas* (From Banning to Moving Ahead)'.

2. 'Child Rights and Child Protection through Community Development – National and State level Consultation – A report 5 October–18 December 2007'.
3. 'Protecting Children in India – A Proposal for the Eleventh Five Year Plan (2007–12). Based on consultation with 287 Child Protection NGOs and Children's Voices, June–July 2006'.

These publications present the outcome of a series of consultations held at regional, state and national level with 287 NGOs and 140 children from 17 NGOs of Delhi and Rajasthan. The objective of these consultations was to facilitate feedback to the child rights related policies in the governments 11th Five Year Plan and thus to enforce children's rights.

Partnerships/Cooperation with other NGO's

Butterflies has a large network and collaborates with a number of NGOs, mostly in the area of children's rights. The NGO also partners with NGOs in the South Asian region in the Children's Development Bank project. The bank has 12 branches in Delhi and now plans to open branches in other Indian cities as well as Afghanistan, Bangladesh and Nepal in the near future, according to a representative of Butterflies.

Two Butterflies employees are responsible for the alliance programme. Over the years it has built a few networks, such as a children's forum called 'Delhi Child Rights Club' (http://www.butterflieschildrights.org/rightsClub1.asp).

Communication Strategies

Main External Communication Channels

Butterflies has a designated team of two people who are responsible for fundraising and communication. The website contains a plethora of up-to-date information on the NGO's numerous events, workshops and consultations as well as relevant details about Butterflies' strategy, goals and various projects. The website also provides the latest edition of *National Children's Times* and *Delhi*

Children's Times for downloading, and an option to subscribe to receive these copies via email. Interested people also can subscribe to the monthly newsletter.

In addition, among the NGO's key communication channels are regular publications like the quarterly journal *My Name is Today* which contains articles by well-known and highly-regarded experts on children issues along with statistical data and articles published in Indian and foreign newspapers. It is well-received by academic institutions and NGOs. The latest issue of My *Name is Today* is on the theme of Children and HIV/AIDS. Butterflies also publishes, among other things, books on the sexual abuse of children, research reports or studies conducted by the NGO and a comic book on children's rights, which is provided to schools for free. The latest publication was: 'Poverty and Children in Orissa: Strengthening Government Accountability', a study done by Butterflies in collaboration with Save the Children to understand the situation of children living in poverty. The study was conducted from a sample of 100 families from the poverty-stricken districts of Sambalpur and Sundergarh in Orissa.

The NGO has good relations with the government and also runs a project called 'The Child Line', a help-line service for children in distress, sponsored by the Ministry of Women and Child Development. In addition they run workshops and seminars and provide consultation where they involve the government as well as other NGOs. The Ministry also invites the organization for consultations and for inputs in new policies. Nevertheless, on a case-by-case basis, Butterflies can also object to the government's decisions and conduct rallies or press conferences against policy decisions they do not consider favourable to securing children's rights. The organization uses a large number of additional communication channels like press releases, emails, brochures, posters, events, forums and committees, open sessions, annual lecture series on specific topics like 'children and media' or 'children in poverty', press conferences, rallies, website, children's newspapers, alternate media and outreach programmes.

Special Features

The Butterflies websites has several interactive features like the 'Children's Question Corner' or 'NGOs ask us'. While the 'Children's

Question Corner' answers the various questions of children, the latter addresses voluntary development organizations which need input on issues related to child rights and child protection. Organizations can send their queries online and the Butterflies team will provide answers and support.

Main Internal Communication Channels

Butterflies internal communication channels are personal contact, mobile phones, internet and email, regular telephone reporting on the projects, regular reports and fortnightly staff meetings. To ensure communication flow, regular meetings take place, where the reporting is bottom-up: staff members from the various projects/ units report either to their immediate supervisor or to the head of the department and the administrator, while the heads of the programs report to the director.

Campaigns

Butterflies does a lot of internet and local grassroots campaigning, such as open sessions or annual lecture series. Furthermore, to put the rights of children on the agenda of every individual citizen, it has launched a civil society movement called 'I Care for Children', which is basically to enrol normal people as ambassadors for childrens' rights. For a fee of INR 50 ($1) one can join the movement and receive a badge and a booklet of obligations that would identify the person as one who cares about children and who is also available for voluntary service in times of emergencies. Although Butterflies does not measure the success of its campaigns through specific key performance indicators, programmes and yearly objectives are evaluated. The evaluation is mostly done through internal experts, but sometimes with the help of external experts when specific questions are involved.

Advertising/Marketing

Apart from raising awareness, Butterflies' main objectives for advertising are to attract potential employees. To achieve that, the NGO makes intensive use of their website, from which one can send greeting cards or order wooden Amsterdam tulips. Furthermore, brochures and a booklet are given out at every Butterflies event. The Butterflies brochure provides the vision and objectives of the NGO and a brief outline of activities of its various departments. Other publications distributed at the Butterflies' events are *My Name Is Today* and some comic and story books. The *Travelling Twins* series is a comic book which addresses different issues regarding children's rights. *Silver Lining* of the series, for example, which deals with the issue of sexual exploitation in a school setting. *Money Magic* is a comic book depicting how Butterflies helped street and working children in Delhi to start and manage a bank called Children Development Bank (*Bal Vikas* Bank in India) and the benefits that one can derive by being its member. This bank has established in India and other countries in the South Asian region. To sensitize the school children and adults on the issue of child sexual abuse, ARC brought out a fictionalized story book, *You Love Me, You Love Me Not* based on cases Butterflies has handled in the last few years.

Contact

U-4, Green Park Extension, New Delhi – 110 016. India.
Phone: +91-11-2616 3935 or +91-11-2619 1063
Fax: +91-11-2619 6117
Email: butterflies@vsnl.com
Website: http://www.butterflieschildrights.org/home.asp

Chapter Nine

Strategic Communication Planning for NGOs

THE PURPOSE of strategic communication planning is to effectively integrate all the NGO's projects, awareness campaigns and advocacy efforts. This means using corporate communications to create, strengthen, or preserve opinion favourable to the attainment of organizational goals among its target groups. A communication plan is an important part of the daily operation, as it frames all media activities, including internal and external communications, public relations, and clarifies the organization's priorities, target audiences, resources and staff assignments.

By planning and adopting a long-term strategy, you will position yourself to be significantly more proactive and strategic, rather than just reacting to the existing environment. The strategic communication plan helps the organization allocate resources more effectively and more calculatedly by highlighting synergies and opportunities in diverse work areas. The adoption of a communication plan also includes the recognition that all the organization's efforts have a communicational element. In addition to campaigning, an NGO that expects to realize its vision and achieve its mission, also becomes involved in other communicational essentials such as public education, research, public advocacy efforts, networking, providing direct services and fundraising.

A communication plan is driven by the organization's goals and outcomes, its vision as expressed in a mission statement, and its values, beliefs and philosophy. To initiate a successful and effective communication, start with an assessment of your current organizational objectives.

According to the Jossey Bass guide to strategic communication for non-profit organizations, communication goals may include (Bonk et al. 1999):

1. Developing and implementing communications plans for enhanced visibility and/or crisis management.
2. Generating positive media coverage by cultivating relationships with reporters.
3. Increasing the awareness and involvement of specific target groups.
4. Changing attitudes or teaching new skills to staff and volunteers.
5. Generating support from the public, policy-makers and clients for community reforms across the country or globally.
6. Encouraging financial contributions.

The activities in the communication plan should support the organization's overall communication goals such as raising public awareness of one's concerns. It is crucial to set feasible and measurable goals in order to know when they have been achieved and to monitor and gauge the communication process. The objectives have to be SMART:

1. Specific: related to specific outcomes
2. Measurable: quantified
3. Actionable: realistic
4. Relevant: in line with the organization's thrust
5. Timely: related to time frames

In addition to the objectives, vision and values that are fundamental for an NGO's communications strategy, there are six critical elements needed to construct a strategy:

1. Situation Analysis
2. Defining Public

3. Media selection and message development
4. Budget
5. Implementation and control
6. Evaluation

It is crucial to think about these topics before implementing day-to-day activities. Therefore research, as it has already been defined above, is necessary as a base for decision making in the planning process.

Situation Analysis

First of all the NGO has to research the current situation of the organization. For example, it must consider where it is currently, and what the external perceptions of the organization are. It is important to consider the differences among the external image, the NGO's self-perceived image and the image to which the organization aspires. To assess those, one might use the survey techniques previously described; awareness tracking or desk research. Thereafter, one needs to know how the public perceives the NGO and its cause. Media analysis, for example, can be a helpful and cost-effective tool and will give one's your campaign. Furthermore one has to consider the past, present or possible future criticisms, the financial situation and community relations.

Defining Public

The second task is to identify your target groups. Who are your most important stakeholders and how can they be reached? Stakeholders and target groups may include donors, potential members, volunteers, politicians, international or trans-national organizations, opinion makers, religious groups, as well as the legal community, business companies, other NGOs and the general public. In addition to these important external groups, it is important for the organization not to forget its internal audiences, such as staff, volunteers and board members.

Media Selection and Message Development

The next step is choosing the appropriate media channels to meet one's objectives and the target audiences so as to better devise a successful media mix.

It is important to be able to tell reporters how the NGO wants to be perceived. The term 'elevator pitch' refers to a two to four line press release document describing what you want to achieve and how it will be done. If this is not made, you take the chance that journalists might create profiles that may not be accurate. For a start, to describe the organization you should develop frequently asked questions (FAQs) document that can be used anytime, anywhere and with everyone. Furthermore, one should develop key points for the organization's spokespeople to use when they talk to the media. The development and production of high-quality public relation's materials are also important tools to reach journalists, donors, policy-makers and other stakeholders. These should include:

1. A consistent and easy to recognize logo and stationery design.
2. An easy to understand, one page fact sheet about the organization.
3. At least one press kit on the issues and activities to be highlighted in the media.
4. Hard copy brochures and consistent website content.
5. Videos, slides and computer presentations.
6. Research reports and studies for public release as news items.
7. Biographies on spokespeople and agency heads.
8. Copies of the current newsletter, if there is one.
9. Copies of newspaper articles about the organization.

Budget

Carefully estimate the workload, material and expenses you need and develop a cost control plan, which includes an objective-led budget and spells out how resources will be allocated, including staff and volunteer time, computers, software, equipment, databases, in-house and contract services, and so on. In case of NGOs with fewer than 10 employees, where everyone from the director to the person who answers the phone, should be a part of the communications team, for mid-sized to large organizations, it is advisable to hire a communications director. A resource review for the organization should do the following:

1. Assess staff and volunteer time, in-house services and existing media technologies.
2. Recommend and arrange for training and technology updates as needed.
3. Designate or hire a communications director.
4. Develop a budget that includes provisions for external contracts and services, such as freelance writing, database management, graphic design and website management.
5. Assess funding and build programmes for expanded activities that include executive loan programmes, internships, *pro bono* support from commercial media firms, donations from local and regional corporations and grants from foundations.

Implementation and Control

Organizations should develop action plans for each major activity and try to review overall plans at least quarterly. Elements of a communications action plan should spell out assignments and important tasks such as:

1. The development of timelines, calendars of events and priorities.
2. Delegation of responsibilities for leading and supporting staff, giving each a list of specific tasks.
3. A progress review and the enforcement or revision of deadlines.
4. Holding people responsible for completing their work and then reassigning tasks as needed.

Evaluation

Every strategic communications plan needs in-built evaluation components to measure the success of the strategy, to check accountability and, over time, to make improvements. Major evaluation activities might include analyzing media content and monitoring certain developments such as shifts in public opinion, policy changes, increased membership and organizational participation and improved institutional capacity.

Amnesty International has professionalized political communication for NGOs on a global scale.

BEST PRACTICE CASE STUDY: AMNESTY INTERNATIONAL

Mission/Vision

Amnesty International (AI) believes that violation of human rights should be a key concern for the global community. Therefore, AI's key objective is to raise global awareness of human rights violations through governments or societies mainly by campaigning for international solidarity. It defines its mission as:

> [...]to undertake research and action focused on preventing and ending abuses of the rights to physical and mental integrity, freedom of conscience and expression, and freedom from discrimination, within the context of its work to promote all human rights. (Amnesty International in a telephonic interview with Sarah Bastgen, April 2008)

The AI vision can best be summarized by its objectives to stop violence against women, to defend the rights and dignity of those trapped in poverty, to help abolish the death penalty, to oppose torture and terror with the universal principle of justice, to make the case for releasing prisoners of conscience, to protect the rights of refugees and migrants and to regulate the global arms trade.

Approach

AI is an NGO which operates at the global level. Research plays a key role in AI's approach to provide evidence for the issues addressed. In its own words, its approach to fighting for human rights is as follows:

> Working with and for individuals globally, we campaign in a way that potentially each and every person may enjoy all of the human rights enshrined in the Universal Declaration of Human Rights. We undertake research and take action aimed at preventing and ending severe violations of these rights, demanding governments across the globe as well other influential

and powerful institutions and stakeholders respect the rule of law. Consequently, we campaign globally and locally wherever we can make a difference. (Amnesty International in a telephonic interview with Sarah Bastgen, April 2008)

AI's members, volunteers and supporters exert influence on governments, political bodies, companies and inter-governmental groups. Activists address human rights issues by mobilizing public attention and pressure through mass demonstrations, and special activities such as vigils as well as directing lobbying and online campaigning.

Key Success Factors

First and foremost, a key success factor and differentiator to be considered as a valuable source of information and distinctive, reliable knowledge is political neutrality. This was of crucial importance especially during the Cold War until the early 1990s, because AI publicized violations of human rights both in the East and the West. This has been quite a challenge over and over again. The former USSR alleged that AI conducted espionage, the Moroccan government denounced it as a defender of lawbreakers, and the Argentine government banned AI's 1983 annual report.

A further success factor is the proven reliability of information. To ensure all information is reviewed on the 'four eyes principle', all information has to be confirmed and echoed by at least one other credible source. A third factor is AI's global organizational structure, which allows the NGO to operate and act on a global scale. The organization was awarded the 1977 Nobel Peace Prize for its 'campaign against torture' and the UN Human Rights Prize in 1978. AI has human rights subsidiaries globally, which are organized in a democratically-run country-based unit structure.

Background

Amnesty was founded in 1961 in London by the British lawyer Peter Benenson. The German section (situated in Berlin and Bonn) was founded by the German journalists Carola Stern and Gerd Ruge in the same year.

AI is organized democratically throughout its entire structure. The international office in London is in charge of strategic planning and recommends options for initiatives and campaigns targeted at increasing membership. Several times a year, these recommendations are discussed at regular meetings of the board of directors. Communication is organized top–down with directors communicating the outcomes to their own sections. The sections then communicate these outcomes to their local districts which hand them over to the groups within the respective districts. However, decisions are not delegated top–down. Moreover, decisions are 'queried' bottom–up, which might lead to a change of the original decision. The members' positions are aggregated by the Office of the Sections (*Sekretariat der Sektion*) and passed on to the London headquarters. This can be considered as a bottom–up, top–down process of re-evaluating strategic priorities, thus allowing the sections to remain relatively autonomous and not have to implement recommendations from the London headquarters entirely. They are able to pick and choose those which they consider of importance to the specific section.

Amnesty International, Germany

The main body of decision making is the board of management consisting of seven members, the chairman, treasurer, management officers for specified tasks such as public relations or finance, who do this work on a non-profit basis. Apart from that, there is the secretary-general, the business management and department heads, who can be considered the equivalent of full time employees. However, the annual general meeting has the highest relevance and can potentially be the basis for a revision of these decisions. Despite the fact that AI's key objective is to strive for maintaining a consistent image, the autonomy of the members can be considered sacrosanct.

Members/Volunteers

Globally, AI has more than 2.2 million members and subscribers in more than 150 countries and regions, which is centrally coordinated to act for justice on a wide range of issues. AI Germany only has 50 employees, which is supported by a large number of volunteers on the community level. In 2008 approximately 100,000 volunteers and members supported AI Germany.

The main objective of the administrative body is to support the voluntary one. The volunteers get involved in every part of the organization, for example, in country groups, operating at country level; in special topic groups, campaigns, committees or action groups as well as individual case groups, supporting one specific prisoner. Members might decide themselves in which area of focus they want to engage (according to personal interest, language skills or personal contacts with people in a certain region of the world). On the other hand, the NGO strives towards combining expertise and therefore tries to get volunteers involved with certain special groups reflecting their acquired skills. Additionally, on a regular basis, AI offers thematic or country-specific education and training in the areas of membership promotion, financial development and strategic development. These are published in the internal section of the *AI Journal*. There are both internal workshops and seminars which usually take place in cooperation with other partners.

Fundraising

The budget of AI Germany is €11 million.

Sponsors

Since AI is and wants to remain an independent NGO, it does not accept any funding from governments, foundations or political parties and is funded completely through membership fees or individual donations.

Governance

AI is largely made up of voluntary members but retains a small number of paid professionals. In countries where AI has a strong presence, members are organized into 'sections'. In countries where their presence is limited, organizations are built as 'structures', which are aspiring sections. They also coordinate basic activities but have a smaller membership and a limited staff. In countries where no section or structure exists, people can become 'international members'. The organizations outlined above are represented by the International Council (IC) which is led by the IC Chairperson. Members of sections and structures have the right to appoint one or more representatives to the council according to the size of their membership.

The International Executive Committee (IEC), led by the IEC Chairperson, consists of eight members and the IEC Treasurer. It is elected by, and represents, the IC and meets bi-annually. The role of the IEC is to take decisions on behalf of AI, implement the strategy laid out by the IC, and ensure compliance with the organization's statutes.

The German section is formed by 600 community groups. In addition, there are 14,000 individual members and 54,000 donors. Furthermore, although not highly institutionalized, there is a close cooperation among the German, Austrian and Swiss sections because of the shared language. This collaboration is manifested in the joint publication of articles in the respective *AI Journal*. Partial, cross-border group supervision takes place, in which one group is supported by another experienced group. In addition, close cooperation, through exchange of information and experiences also exists with other neighbouring countries such as France, Netherlands and Poland. Last, but not the least, specific national sections, for example in the new democracies in eastern Europe, are supported by specific AI sections.

Networking

Partnerships/Cooperation with other NGOs

AI cooperates with other human rights organizations in order to create synergies, to appear as a 'single voice' to the public as well as to potentially share financial resources. Smaller NGOs can especially benefit from cooperation with AI, since it is the organization with the largest financial resources (at least in Germany). Many of these relationships can form long-term partnerships such as the Forum for Human Rights which is a combination of about 60 NGOs. Because of different objectives, these organizations often only cooperate to some extent. Furthermore AI is also part of short-term action alliances for special issues and is a member of the Platform for Civil Conflict Management (*Plattform für zivile Konfliktbearbeitung*). In addition to its public presence as a union to increase pressure, the objective of cooperation is to achieve a division of labour and to profit from the expertise of other NGOs.

Communication Strategy

AI uses a variety of communication strategies. For one, as an organization purely based on individual membership, a special focus is placed on active members. The NGO is dependent on members acting as ambassadors of AI's objectives in their respective ecosystem. For example, to present and disseminate information on a weekend at a booth at a farmers' market, to give speeches, visit schools to educate and elucidate on human rights, or to engage in solemn vigils in front of embassies. AI also presents a significant media presence through PR and campaigning, both at regional and the national levels. Furthermore, the NGO capitalizes on an effective campaigning team which works upon the information AI Germany receives from the London headquarters and presents it in a way which allows the individual members to react upon them quickly. One example is 'urgent actions' through which AI mobilizes support globally for political prisoners by having individuals send letters to the respective government.

External Communication Channels

One of the main communication vehicles is the report on the 'State of the World's Human Rights', which is published on an annual basis. The report is sold and adds to AI revenues. Apart from that, press releases are used whenever an issue needs to be addressed in real time and disseminated more broadly. Furthermore, AI has built up a network of supporting journalists over the years and maintains close contacts with them, so as to ensure the flow of information to those who focus on special subjects, such as refugee rights or those who are interested in a certain region of the world. In addition, there are background conversations with the press in which the journalists are briefed on a special or hot topic such as was done in the spring of 2008 regarding the protests around the Olympic Games in China.

Moreover, AI is also present at events such as the international book fair in Frankfurt (*Frankfurter Buchmesse*) or the film festival *Berlinale*. At the latter, AI awards The Human Rights Award to a movie addressing the topic of human rights. In this way AI not only tries to raise attention about its own issues, encourages other people to engage in human rights as well. In sum, AI uses press releases, press statements, press conferences, and the publication of records and reports, predominantly written by AI country experts based in the International Office in London.

Other communication channels apart from the website include:

1. the AI Jounal (6 issues per year);
2. an email newsletter on the latest news;
3. urgent actions and press releases, actions by members;
4. mailing actions initiated by the fundraising unit;
5. events on cultural and political basis as well as lobbying towards ministries and companies.

In order to address governments and political authorities AI makes use of urgent action 'Letters against Oblivion', whereby members and other interested people around the globe are encouraged to publicly show solidarity for a certain political prisoner. This action has been very successful, since one must not underestimate the impression made in some countries by the arrival of letters and faxes from all over the world, advocating in favour of a particular political prisoner. In 2008 Rebiya Kadeer, a political prisoner in China was released after more than five years in prison due to AI 'urgent action' letters from across the globe.

In addition, AI lobbies the Ministry of Foreign Affairs, the Parliament, especially the Committee of Foreign Affairs, the Committee of Human Rights and the Committee of Defence and partly the Committee for the Interior which is responsible for questions pertaining to refugee policy. AI tries to inform members of the parliament and ministers should there be a need to journey to a specific country and/or to have talks to clarify its concerns and/or appeal to have them communicated further to the political authorities in said country. In addition, AI employs its own lobbyists who contact the state parliaments. In a more confined scope, large companies are addressed if AI thinks that these companies could support them.

Internal Communication Channels

One of the most important internal communication channels is the intranet for registered members in order to exchange information and campaign materials such as flyers or posters. Other successful communication channels are the 'Amnesty Intern' section in the AI Journal, which serves as an internal discussion and contribution forum and is only sent to members. Apart from that, members are regularly updated through mail. Furthermore, AI in Germany is divided into 600 separate groups organized in regional districts which hold regular conferences to provide opportunities for exchanging information and discussing particular issues. Other opportunities for internal discussions are the district speakers' conference (the most important decision making committee between the meetings that take place quarterly) and the annual meeting of all members. To ensure the flow of communication the elected functionaries are responsible for and obliged to report at the regional area conference.

Research Concerning the Communication Efforts

Both at the voluntary and the in-house levels there are various working groups formed by AI internal experts who are responsible for communication planning. Approximately every two years, AI formulates an international strategic plan as well as a national operational plan. In the national operational plan the set strategic goals are broken down to the national level.

On a regular basis the campaigning unit conducts analyses in order to gather information on how to communicate certain messages or, retrospectively, how to improve the communications, that is, what worked out well, what did not and what could be improved the next time.

Campaigning

AI initiates permanent and topical or case specific campaigns and activities. The type of campaigning depends heavily on the specifics and the campaign objectives. For this reason, the NGO initiates two kinds of campaigns – those lasting approximately three months, and others which last over several years such as the campaign against sexual harassment (Stop Violence against Women), which has been running for more than a decade. Following up on an individual case such as one involving a political prisoner can sometimes last up to 15 years until the goal is met. The majority of the campaigns, however, take place within a year.

Generally, in a year, one to two significantly large campaigns run parallel to two to three smaller ones. On specific days such as the Day of Human Rights, the International Women's Day or the Day of the Refugee, short-term actions in the form of readings, street campaigning or other events take place. One the most successful ways of campaigning is the urgent action network using letters and faxes in combination with lobbying the Ministry of Foreign Affairs; articles in the AI Journal and interviews in national newspapers achieve a success rate of up to 70 per cent. Those actions also form the bigger part of the campaigning quantitatively. Concerning issues of low salience to the public, for example, judicial subtleties in the protection of refugees, AI often resorts to the classic, traditional form of lobbying.

Evaluation of Campaigns

A campaign is considered successful if a violation of human rights comes to the public fore and has a chance of being corrected. Other success factors defined in the national operative plan are membership and financial growth. As AI often aspires to reach higher grounds, the points mentioned above are often only partially fulfilled.

AI tries to measure the success of its campaigns/actions or at least thoughtfully reviews parts of the campaign which are considered to have been a success. Often though, the corresponding performance indicator cannot be quantified so, the success of the campaign cannot always be measured precisely. Their campaigning is targeted towards policy change which they have initiated quite successfully in a number of cases. At the inter-governmental level AI pressed for application of the UN's Standard Minimum Rules for the Treatment of Prisoners and of existing humanitarian conventions; lobbied to secure ratifications of the two UN Covenants on Human Rights (which came into force in 1976) and was instrumental in obtaining UN Resolution 3059 which formally denounced torture and called on governments to adhere to existing international instruments and provisions forbidding its practice. Consultative status was granted at the Inter-American Commission on Human Rights in 1972.

Marketing/Advertising

Public relations and campaigning efforts are tools to influence policy making, but there are also attempts to attract new members, to promote AI and to mobilize financial support. Thus the most important tools are public relations in general; for example, press conferences, press releases, events, membership promotion initiated by members and the AI journal.

Stakeholders

AI is purely a membership organization and receives financial support only from its members. Thus, members and donors play an important role. Communication is mainly targeted towards members, although there are different channels of communication, and, of course, a variety of topics. As an example, a circular letter including a brief statement and a request for active or financial support are sent to all members and donors three times per year.

Communications with other stakeholders, such as refugees, demand other channels, platforms and contents. This could include, for example roundtable discussions concerning a certain issue.

Contact

53108 Bonn
Telephone: 0228/9 83 73-0
Fax: 0228/63 00 36
E-mail: info@amnesty.de
Website: http://www2.amnesty.de/amnesty international Sektion der Bundesrepublik Deutschland e.V.

MARKETING THE ISSUE

By applying the methodologies already introduced, there are a number of core marketing tools which can be used. Overall, success is about understanding the market and defining the positioning of the organization, as we have done as a start to formulating our strategy. Apart from that, you need to 'sell' your product or idea accordingly, and applying the marketing mix can help you with this.

What is the 'product' one wants to sell? The marketing mix is probably the most renowned phrase in marketing and was coined by Neil H. Borden in his 1965 article 'The Concept of the Marketing Mix', which provides a framework for analysing the strategic competitive position in terms of its marketing strength. Marketing has developed a number of powerful tools to position or 'sell' an organization, as illustrated in Table 9.1.

The elements of the mix are the marketing 'tactics', also known as the 'Four Ps':

1. Product
2. Price
3. Place
4. Promotion

FIGURE 9.1
Overview of Core Marketing Processes

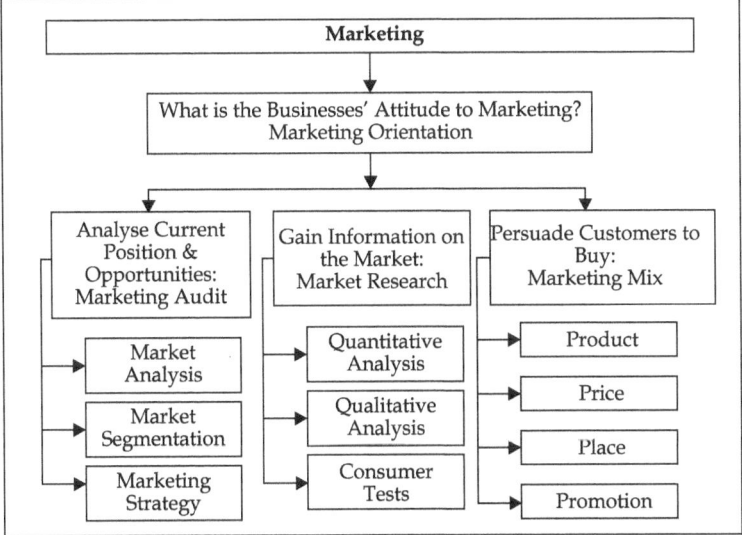

Source: Hovland (2005).

The framework takes the view of the customer, (that is, the donor) to come up with a decision on how to approach the public sphere. (Hovland and Start 2004: 38) explain the applicability for the non-profit world:

> In the think tank world of policy influence the concept [of the four Ps] is still useful and particularly so when considering the promotional strategy. In planning the message, we have considered the product (the content of the message, or the issue), the physical evidence (the credentials to back up the message, or the research) and the price (how politically controversial the message will be, or the position). In planning for the policy audience, we considered the people (the policy audience we are communicating with).

CAMPAIGNING

A campaign will help you influence public opinion and policy formulation. The objective of campaigning is to mobilize the political will to change policies. Typically, it addresses the heart and appeals to the emotions of the audience. Pitt et al. (2005) have come up with a number of recommendations that are needed to make a campaign successful:

1. 'The political context is the critical issue that campaigners need to assess in advance. Campaigns need to seize windows of opportunity to have optimum impact. Since the political context is continuously changing, campaigns also need to work with models of institutional change.

2. The complexity of policy processes has to be considered when planning a campaign. Whilst campaigns are generally successful in setting the political agenda, effective strategies need to be developed to encourage implementation. Such strategies could help to bridge the trade-off between short-term political pressure and long-term implementation success. It is most effectively done by establishing cooperative relations with those institutions responsible for implementation, to ensure that the vital political infrastructure is in place.

3. Relevant and credible evidence influences policy processes. Both research-based evidence and policy-advocacy research can be relevant and credible, but need to be utilized appropriately depending on the objective of the campaign.

4. Effective communication of evidence is critical. The simplicity of the narrative on which the argument is based, and attractiveness of the policy associated with it, is vital to the success of a campaign. The communication strategy must be according to the needs of its audience: the general public is more responsive to easily understood messages with a strong political angle, whilst politicians are more responsive to technical solution-orientated reports. To maintain the momentum of a campaign, regular annual events and a focus on key policy summits may prove more effective than consistent efforts throughout.

5. Networks are important for increasing the legitimacy of a campaign, both within the public eye and among politicians, and can be used to create a 'boomerang' effect. Links with influential individuals can help to 'open windows' or increase a campaign's profile. Systematic capacity building can also enable international institutions to communicate more effectively with CSOs, as the campaign's

Secretariat can act as a point of contact. To avoid the break down of a coalition, the agendas and terms of NGO partnerships should be explicitly set out and priorities negotiated among NGOs involved (Pitt et al. 2005).

Based on the stakeholder analysis and power mapping exercise, POCA has understood who the key decision makers are in their respective policy field. They have decided to take a three step approach:

1. POCA has conducted in depth research for their internal needs. Discussion with subject matter experts from other NGOs and policy-makers in ministries and international organizations have proven that they have collected data which is of wider interest. They publish a study together with a university which has a very high reputation in this policy field. The study is launched at a public event where the Minister for Youth is giving a keynote speech.
2. POCA has decided to launch a campaign to raise the awareness in the population for the wider issue. Thankfully a PR agency has decided to donate the work of their campaign specialist to this.
3. POCA has signed up to participate in roundtables and expert networks where the issue is discussed.

---

iCONGO, the Indian Confederation of NGOs has developed a very sophisticated approach to market their main objective. A mixture of public relations, conferences and advocacy has helped iCONGO to engage their key stakeholders.

BEST PRACTICE CASE STUDY: iCONGO

Mission/Vision

The Indian Confederation of NGOs, iCONGO is a confederation of NGOs, consisting of around 80 members. Having started with 155 NGOs, iCONGO over the years has downsized to around 80 NGOs as they only want absolutely transparent and accountable NGOs with huge integrity and commitment to the cause as members. iCONGO has, over the years, with citizen involvement at every level, become the hallmark and gateway for philanthropy in India. Various NGOs now want to become members, albeit membership is granted only after pre-screening and in-depth study of the applicant. iCONGO's core charter is to promote social justice through citizen action and social responsibility – a pioneering concept again, as it goes beyond funds and asks people not just to give but to practice philanthropy for social justice, where individuals get involved with a cause, understand the social issues and thus become the change by advocating for the cause. Its main objectives are promoting ideas of social inclusion and justice in Indian society, and making the case for giving back to each member of society. iCONGO also operates as a form of clearinghouse, applying rigorous criteria for member organizations. It also supports NGOs in India by providing public platforms for their social cause, by professionalizing its outreach and by improving communication. In a nutshell, it strives to address the large Indian middle class which intends to support charities or NGOs but lacks the understanding for assessing which organizations are trustworthy. iCONGO links up supporters with credible, transparent and accountable NGOs. The organization's vision is to make iCONGO the hub of the social and development sector in India, and achieve a quantum leap in funds raised for NGOs. It also wants to provide its member NGOs with a common infrastructure, to help to decrease operative costs and to improve operational efficiency. iCONGO believes that the basis for ensuring inclusive growth and justice in the Indian society is based on civil society, with NGOs helping to address, aggregate and channel civic engagement.

Approach

iCONGO's main approach is to bring innovations to the non-profit sector, enabling them to work with the civil society. To achieve this, it works globally with stakeholders in the Indian society, international organizations and corporations. Some of its innovative approaches include launching the first big donor loyalty program, *Karm Mitra*, and sensitizing top executives in corporate India through an award-winning film *The Joy of Giving*. This film accented the plight of communities such as the Dalits, tribals, commercial sex workers, manual scavengers, homeless and disabled as well as people affected by riots and communal violence — a model that is now benefiting various charities who have adopted this approach. The founders of iCONGO also pioneered the concept of face-to-face fundraising in India with *Karm Mitra* and created a network of direct sales agencies that promoted social justice investment through a team of fundraising and social investment consultants. This team was trained to sensitize people to social and poverty-related issues. Other than its main aim (to sensitize people) iCONGO works towards building an ecosystem for the NGO sector, for ethical fundraising and holistic development by involving citizens as friends in action for social justice. The fund though was secondary, the primary objective being the awakening and enlightenment of the people into a so-called 'India Shining' about the plight of un-served and under-served communities, which were victims of chronic hunger and impoverishment. The idea is to reclaim and preserve public trust in the people sector (that is, the NGOs) and thus iCONGO pre-screens and audits NGO members through an audit firm based on the Omega ratings which have been designed in consultation with citizen supporters.

The founders of iCONGO pioneered the concept of 'media for change' and produced and promoted the first big Bollywood issue-based movie concerning the dignity of people with HIV/AIDS in India, titled *Ek Alag Mausam*. It featured Nandita Das, Anupam Kher, Rajat Kapur and became a model for other movies like *Phir Milenge*, *My Brother Nikhil*, *Black* and so on. Furthermore, iCONGO, along with Channel V and MTV, promoted the first music video, *Khushhi — the Joy of Giving*, on children and community rights for youth involvement.

Since mid-2005, the founders of iCONGO have been conducting workshops for NGOs across the country (even for non-members) to promote ethical practices in fundraising and to safeguard the long-term interests of the entire sector. iCONGO works with NGOs to promote long-term ethical fundraising where its not about just chasing money but about creating citizen involvement. iCONGO works with citizens to tell them to not just give but make a social justice investment by getting involved with the cause, understanding the issues and advocating against social wrongs; in short, To Be The Change.

iCONGO has conducted over 50 such workshops and various citizen forums and helped formulate strategies for various international and grassroots NGOs. Most of these workshops have received overwhelming response and reviews as the best fundraising, social and cause-related marketing and communications training programmes. iCONGO has also been approached by various firms such as Bharti, DLF, Allianz, Yum Foods and various others to help them create their CSR strategy. iCONGO has also been approached by GE Money to be its knowledge partners for a consumer education website to promote responsible borrowing and financial management. In 2008, iCONGO partnered with Population First and UNFPA (UN Population Fund) to promote the *Laadli* awards for gender sensitivity in media companies and advertising agencies.

Background

The iCONGO formal documents were put together in New Delhi on 26 November 2004, even though its organizational history goes back to 2003, when their founders started to engage various stakeholders on their concept for building a confederation.

Organizational Structure

The organization has a flat structure and participatory decision-making. Decisions are made collectively by all the people working in the organization. These are then discussed and approved by the governing board, which includes people from all sectors, or the managing committee. Currently iCONGO is in the process of forming an advisory board.

In addition, the NGO has three paid citizen volunteers who work for a comparatively low honorarium, as iCONGO wants to keep administration cost minimal.

Members and Volunteers

As iCONGO is a network consisting of NGOs, it does not have any individual members, but a large base of volunteers who give their time and support for a variety of occasions. Individuals who have taken up this mission proactively are labelled as 'honorary directors'. The volunteers are an integral part of the organi-zation and therefore participate in all areas of the organization's activities.

Partnership with other NGOs

The organization collaborates with all types other NGOs, but generally with small grassroots-level NGOs, working hands-on with the communities. The collaboration is not a permanent one, but a loose confederation with collective infrastructure and a consultancy centred at iCONGO.

Fundraising

The NGO neither accepts grants nor takes donations from or-ganizations, institutions, individuals, and so on. iCONGO is a membership-driven organization and collects money from a fixed membership fee. The NGO raises money through earned revenues from sponsorships for various forums that they conduct (for example, The Knowledge Forum), CSR and cause-related marketing. It considers itself as a service provider whose revenue is related to the value created. iCONGO also consults with various companies for CSR strategy and conceptualizing and designing cause related marketing activities. iCONGO facilitates funds and resources for various member NGOs without retaining any percentage from funds raised and facilitated and is the first organization in the world to do so absolutely selflessly. Over the past four years iCONGO has selflessly raised over 150 million INR for various causes and is now creating gateways like cause payroll, cause online, cause direct, restaurants against hunger to get people involved with small but very credible and efficient NGOs.

Main Communication Strategies

The iCONGO communication strategy is geared towards increasing the number of partners. It tries to have as many partnerships as possible. It partners with organizations which have their events, in order to spread awareness about various causes. It leverages every opportunity through branding, long term media partnerships, cross-sectoral partnerships and the like. It also has its annual Right Every Wrong conclave in which it deals with particular and prominent social issues. For those, it invites eminent speakers from various sectors (NGO, corporate, government, media, academia, and so on).

Main External Communication Channels

iCONGO's main communication channel is the media, for example, the iCONGO Media Service (IMS) through which it provides its member NGOs with a fundraising channel at low, discounted rates. The organization has also launched a 24/7 media news portal www. dishoooom.com. Here, not only NGOs, but every member of civil society in India can contribute to and share his or her views on any social topic or issue. iCONGO also uses direct mailing and manages a database of around 500,000 email addresses. Overall, the main communication channels include the internet—in particular the websites www.icongo.in and www.righteverywrong.com—print media, letters, the citizen website Dishoooom and a network of advisors and mentors. iCONGO avoids too much print material to save costs related to futile printing and to save the trees.

Main Internal Communication Channels

All the communication channels mentioned above are also used for internal communication. In annual meetings the reporting of various member NGOs such as Right Every Wrong, takes place, where iCONGO has a 360 degree feedback session on their mentorship, advisory council and citizen volunteers.

Research on Communication Effectiveness

iCONGO does a lot of research regarding its communication efforts including questions like:

1. Which other organizations focus on my policy field?
2. Does it make sense from a financial perspective to focus on the same field?
3. With whom can I partner to leverage and add value to the entire effort without replication?
4. What is the public perception of the sector and how do citizens view the sector?
5. What are the social involvement or giving practices in India and how can the ecosystem be created or improved for preserving public trust in the sector and long-term sustainability?

Campaigning

For iCONGO, the most successful tools for campaigning are email broadcasts, its citizen action media portal www.dishoooom.com, and media partnerships. iCONGO's campaigning is always issue-related and takes up different topics at different points in time. But the organization's continuous focus is to motivate citizens of India to involve themselves proactively with various causes, so as to bring about a change in the society. To achieve their objectives, iCONGO mostly initiates grassroots campaigns through awareness and knowledge forums as well as media campaigns.

Assessment of Campaigns

The success of its campaigns is measured by evaluating the impact they had on various people regarding the changing of their actions and behaviour. This can be clearly seen through the follow-up work taken up by various people after the campaigns. Recently at the REW Conclave, for example, the focus was climate change. It was attended by a lot of people from various parts of the country with many of these people returning to their states and starting small projects to combat climate change. This was done in coordination with iCONGO and the NGO was delighted to see that a lot of people joined as volunteers and pledged to work in their areas to bring about awareness and to involve other people proactively. These small contributions will actually lead to waves of change that will definitely have a positive impact on the larger picture. iCONGO's for a and campaigns have also led to other organizations and companies adopting iCONGO ideas for their campaigns.

Marketing

The most successful marketing tools are media partnerships and a policy-related approach. The organization approaches people and, instead of just perfunctorily asking for advertisements or other public relations ideas, involves them in various causes. The marketing strategy is low cost as, by design, iCONGO has no budget for marketing. It prefers to use the little money at its disposal for effective and impactful campaigning. However, because of its philosophy and ideals it has had long-term media support from TV channels, press and online media which promote the organization's various forums and campaigns. iCONGO believes in the power of ideas and innovation to create cutting-edge campaign strategies, which the organization then presents to potential partners. In addition it utilizes the online citizen and NGO media news portal www.dishoooom.com, which is the first of its kind and which reaches out to over half a million people. It uses this medium effectively to promote campaigns, online giving and shopping. Through this medium, iCONGO is also creating corporate 'founder subscribers' who invest in advertising on the portal. In lieu of advertising and branding, all forums and campaigns are supported by organizations, on a purely sponsorship model.

Stakeholders

The organization's most important stakeholders include the entire citizen sector comprising youth, NGOs, corporations, SMEs, the government and other similar groups. In its marketing efforts, iCONGO focuses on both customer relationship management as well as the stakeholder relationship management.

Contact

Indian Confederation of NGOs
184 Belvedere Park, DLF Phase 3
Gurgaon, Haryana 122002
India.
Website: http://www.icongo.in/

Advocacy

*One person with a belief is a social power equal
to ninety-nine who have only interests.*

John Stuart Mill

A DVOCACY ACTIVITIES can include a number of different things like public education, campaigns to influence public opinion; research for interpretation of problems and suggesting preferred solutions; constituent action and public mobilizations; agenda setting and policy design, lobbying; policy implementation, monitoring, and feedback and election-related activity. However, there is no agreement on which activities constitute advocacy (Reid 2000). Basically, through advocacy one is identifying, embracing and promoting a cause, shaping public opinion, and championing the interests of one's community.

Advocacy, with lobbying being the famous sub-segment of it, is the supreme discipline required on one's way to initiating policy change. Advocacy can be both confrontational or diplomatic, targeted to interact with decision makers in order to initiate change. Advocacy tools include:

1. Media.
2. Lobbying.
3. Grassroots mobilization.
4. The building of coalitions or alliances.
5. The utilization of the legal system.

Using such methods and channels typically results in a change in legislation, the most famous example being the women's movement which, of course, brought about voting rights, and the legally-binding, guaranteed equal opportunities for a woman to choose a career. Another example would be the anti-whaling campaign in Australia, which resulted in the passing of the Whale Protection Act, 1980 (Gray 2006).

David Cohen, Co-Director of the Advocacy Institute, defined advocacy as,

> [consisting] of organized efforts and actions that use the instruments of democracy to establish and implement laws and policies that will create a just and equitable society. These instruments include elections, mass mobilization, civil action (including civil disobedience), lobbying, negotiations, bargaining and court action. (Transition Monitoring Group 2006: 5)

The different tools:

1. Using Media
    Through effective use of media you can set your topic on the public agenda so as to create the deal with it. Of course, your information needs to be timely, topical, relevant and reliable. It has to be published at a time where public attention is not distracted by major events such as national elections or a natural catastrophe. Only well-known NGOs get requests by media when there is a need for commentary on a specific happening in their respective policy field. In most cases, to trigger publication, one has to contact the media. Ideally, you work through contacts that position a story with a journalist. If one happens to be a 'no–name' and cannot immediately be identified as a reliable source of information, it will not get you anywhere. There is an art to developing good media relations and it should not be done ad hoc.

    Here are some tips on becoming a resource for journalists:

    (a) Be available. Give reporters, especially those at news services where they work odd hours, your home and mobile numbers and tell them that it is permissible to call you.

(b) Seek out journalists at meetings and other gatherings and give them your business card.

(c) Be ready to be quoted. Having to call back once the quote has been cleared will reduce the chance of the quotation being used.

(d) Know the issues. Read and comment intelligently on developments relating to your cause.

(e) Do not always assume journalists have received the same information you have about topical events or relevant news releases.

(f) Avoid rhetoric and ideological arguments; most journalists have heard all this before.

(g) Know your facts; never pass on information unless you know it is true and verifiable.

(h) Know where to find information or contacts fast, thereby gaining a reputation as a good source.

(i) Getting into the papers requires more than just having good relations (Calamann 1998).

2. Lobbying

We can distinguish between direct lobbying, which is communication with a legislator who attempts to influence specific legislation, from indirect lobbying, which is urging others to adopt a stated position on specific legislation and voicing a call to action (Smucker 1999). Lobbying is about informing key decision makers, and 'persuading' them by showing the added value of a policy change. The prerequisite for using this tool is, obviously, access to key people; however, one also needs to be able to show evidence for the case one is presenting. This has to be based on fact and the strategic research section of this book shows you how to get there. Furthermore, both you and the organization you are representing need to be considered a source of credible and reliable information. It is not only about the facts, but even more importantly about how the message is conveyed. It is important to understand where people are coming from and what is driving their decision-making processes. If you approach politicians you might need to consider that they are driven by maximizing votes, whereas representatives of corporations are driven by maximizing revenues. It is important to remember that relationships based on mutual respect and shared benefits are very crucial assets. You can only disappoint once—so make sure you present an air-tight case.

3. Mobilizing People at Grassroots

   This can be very powerful for engaging people and increasing the number of voices. Furthermore, it is gives voice to the people: INP+, the Chennai based NGO dealing with HIV/AIDS educates people with this illness to act as 'positive speakers' to help improve prevention and decrease stigmatization of infected people. By speaking openly about their illness in public and engaging with people at the community level, in schools or companies, people thus take ownership of their life and become subjects, rather than objects of their fate. In other words, they achieve dignity.

4. Building Alliances or Coalitions

   Creating synergies and/or increasing the critical mass are paramount objectives for building partnerships. Through these, one is able to leverage networks, and use expertise and the capabilities in other organizations. Nevertheless, there are some challenges. For example, you might want spend more time on defining how you want to work together than actually doing the work. This is particularly true if you are targeting a partnership for a longer period of time. Up front, make sure you understand each other's objectives, ideological affiliations and decision making processes. Define common objectives and ensure a division of labour that does not put too much on one partner's shoulder.

5. Using the Legal System

   This is a tricky and delicate situation, as one has to be very well prepared and must be convinced that one is building a strong case. You have to do some scenario analysis regarding the outcome of the case. Otherwise, you might not only lose a lot of money but your reputation as well. What actually needs to be considered strongly is that filing a lawsuit works best in a country which has a fair juridical system. Using this tool in an autocratic state might be an insurmountable challenge.

The Banyan, the Chennai-based NGO looking after mentally ill, homeless women can be considered a best practice for advocacy. Through joint projects with public institutions in the domains of healthcare and policing, it has changed the way these women are dealt with. Training and building ownership in the public organizations have helped change attitudes and behaviours.

BEST PRACTICE CASE STUDY: THE BANYAN

Vision/Mission

The Banyan began as a humanistic response to the invisible reality of homeless women with mental illness. In its 14 years of operation, The Banyan has responded to the needs of over 2,000 women and reunited over 1,100 women with their families. As an NGO working on rescue, treatment and rehabilitation of mentally ill women, The Banyan has evolved from a non-profit organization into a for-impact organization and their present interventions, mode of operation, systems of treatment, care, community outreach and research support this fact. The Banyan's response has, over the years, evolved from a service delivery organization to an organization that is focused on catalyzing an increase in stakeholders in mental health care for homeless persons.

The vision of The Banyan is to rehabilitate and reintegrate the homeless women who come to them and lack sufficient access to care. Their main goal is to rescue, treat and provide these women training in vocational skills and then reunite them with their families. Furthermore, the organization tries to help them meld into society, allowing them to lead decent, normal and dignified lives. The Banyan believes in the rights of the completely marginalized sections of society — to live and to be. Their vision is 'for a just society in which the rights and needs of the completely marginalized are addressed without exception'. They want to achieve this by acting as a catalyst to increase awareness and acceptance of these issues, create the momentum for government and society to develop appropriate responses. The Banyan campaigns to create the momentum for government and society to develop sustainable policy solutions.

Approach

The Banyan offers a home to homeless, wandering, mentally ill women living in the streets of Chennai. The Banyan is unique in its holistic approach. It has mastered the art of street rescue by being compliant with legal requirements. After rescuing women from the streets, it takes them to a police station, lodges an FIR, takes a court order for treatment, admits them to the government hospital and monitors their treatment and care procedure.

After that, The Banyan continues in pacifying the women, caring for them, getting a court order for treatment, reporting to the psychiatrist to assess the case and begin treatment, documenting details, giving medicines, helping with vocational training, building self-confidence in their clients and finally travelling on rehabilitation trips across India to reunite these women with their families. In mid-2008, The Banyan offered a home and a future to more than 350 women. The NGO provides women with a safe shelter, medical care, psychological counselling and a supportive environment to foster recovery with the aim of the woman taking responsibility for their lives again. After their rehabilitation the organization continues to support the women's return to their families and communities. If this option does not exist, The Banyan supports the women in developing new lives for themselves. One way of doing this is to offer paid jobs either at The Banyan or outside the NGO. Thus the ultimate goal of the organization is rehabilitation and empowerment. If this option does not equate to the women's abilities and needs, the organization provides them with a future in a protected community where they can live as respected members.

Focus areas have been to work for homeless persons with mental illness and persons with low or zero access to care who are at high risk to become homeless, and to increase stakeholders who will advocate this cause.

The fundamental cornerstones of its strategies are:

1. To provide mental health care for the most marginalized. This includes:

   (a) homeless persons with mental illness; and
   (b) persons with mental illness with low or zero access to care who are at high risk to become homeless.

2. To facilitate their journey towards independence and decision-making.
3. To innovate and improve the care and rehabilitation processes and to create multiple client and context-specific responses.
4. To address both ends of the spectrum: from prevention to crisis intervention, leading to rehabilitation.
5. To work with partners to implement, conduct research and advocate.

The Banyan's key goal, to facilitate a journey towards independence (see Table 10.1) whereby clients can make their own choices, dictates all their interventions.

FIGURE 10.1
Facilitating Journey towards Independence and Making Choices

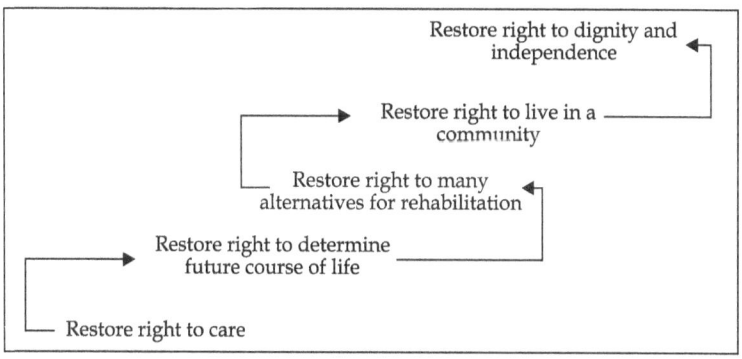

Source: The Banyan. 2008. 'Overview of Activities', July.

Statistics until 2008 support the success of the holistic model:

1. 1,823 women have been admitted so far into The Banyan.
2. 1,101 of these have been re-united with their families across 13 states.
3. 272 of them live in 'Adaikalam' where they undergo treatment and therapy.
4. Ten stay in a group home, geared towards independence.
5. Forty-one live at the Working Women's Hostel.

6. 1,100 draw strength from the security of the Kovalam Health Centre — Commuity Mental Health Programme (CMHP).
7. 1,350 people have benefited through their outreach initiatives in both rural and urban settings.
8. 714 have passed through The Banyan's pioneering mental health helpline — Asia's first such public–private partnership.
9. 235 patients admitted via the Dial 100 programme have been rehabilitated with the help of the Institute of Mental Health and the Chennai Police.
10. 200 management students of reputed management institutes in Chennai have undergone training on 'Leadership and Development' at the Banyan Academy of Leadership in Mental Health (BALM).
11. Eighteen interns from India and abroad have done commendable work at The Banyan and BALM in the last one year.
12. Forty-four students from the Institute of Financial Management and Research (IFMR) have done internship projects for over 6 months at The Banyan and BALM.
13. Research on issues of mental health, advocacy, livelihoods, and so on, is a continual phenomenon at The Banyan and the Banyan Academy of Leadership.

Background

The Banyan was registered as a trust in 1993 in Chennai (Tamil Nadu). In a recent interview the two founders Vandana and Vaishnavi[1] described how it all began:

> We both were students in Chennai and had very clear views on how the development sector should work. We were sure that our theoretical concepts and approaches were the cornerstone and were quick in pointing fingers at others. Then came a day which changed our lives. Leaving school, we found one homeless, close-to-naked obviously-deluded woman on the street; quite alone and screaming for attention and decided to take care of her,

hunting through the streets of Chennai to find a place for her. After futile attempts with various local institutions we figured that there was no place for women who were both homeless and mentally ill to go. However, we finally found a shelter to look after her. We ended the day feeling good about ourselves, only to learn three days later that the woman had run away. We were both 22 years old when this happened, had no idea about mental illness but learnt through that incident that it was not just our academic concepts that would make the difference but what we actually do ourselves on the management of care and rehabilitation in this sector.

The Banyan's organizational structure consists of a board of trustees and two managing trustees who are the two founders: one of them being responsible for projects and fundraising, while the other being in charge of administration and finance (see Table 10.2).

The Banyan's board of trustees consists of 14 persons including a chairperson, a secretary and a treasurer. The board is supposed to meet once every three months, but in practice meets far more often when there are critical decisions (mostly on the policy level) to be taken such as there being a potential funding crisis, a problem with loans, needs for high-level recruitment or the organization of large events. Nevertheless, most of the operational decisions are made within the team which provides suggestions and recommendations; these are then discussed and taken up to the board level. In addition there is a lot of interaction between the staff and the trustees who are directly involved in The Banyan's work.

On a daily basis, the senior coordinators such as the managers and experts of the various programmes are independent in their directions and decisions, but ensure that the operation is according to the framework developed by the board and based on the overall Banyan's vision. All activities of The Banyan are regularly reported to the board. To ensure the flow of communication, there is a two-level system of monitoring and reporting: first the managing trustees review the programmes from time to time; second, the Banyan Academy of Leadership in Mental Health (BALM http://www.balm.in/home.html) makes an objective review of the projects in terms of their goals, leaderships, etc.

FIGURE 10.2

Banyan Organizational Structure

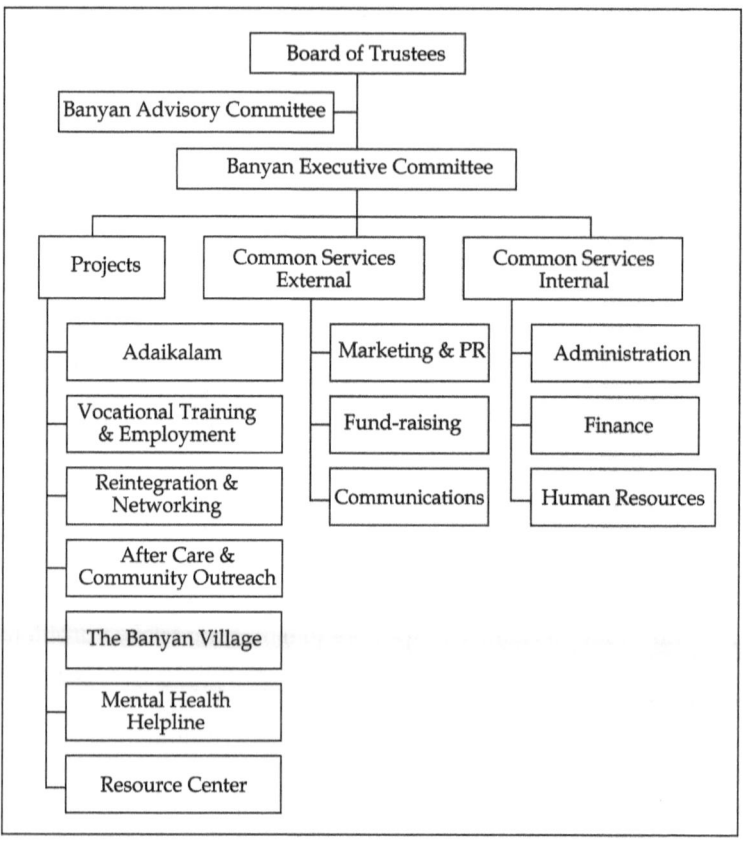

Source: http://www.thebanyan.org/(Accessed in August 2008).

The Banyan has 130 employees, of whom 117 are full-time equivalents and 13 are consultants, working on a project-wise, contractual basis. Furthermore there are approximately 200 volunteers, 50–100 of whom engage with the Banyan regularly in a variety of areas. Because of their special focus on giving their inhabitants a safe home and rehabilitation, the organization does not only need financial support but also any practical, hands-on help available and to spread the idea of The Banyan. Primarily the volunteers are involved in fundraising, internal networking, some work with The Banyan's residents, vocational training and administration-related tasks. The NGO does not have any members who pay fees.

Most Important Stakeholder Groups

The Banyan's most important stakeholder groups are the residents and the mentally ill community members who need help but have no one to voice their concerns.

Another important stakeholder is the government, the communities that they take care of, (inter)national donors, other NGOs, The Banyan team and the general public. However there is no clear hierarchy, but two levels: in the narrow perspective, the government and in a broader perspective, the society and common people.

Funding

The Banyan has operating costs of $856,021 or 36 million INR a year, which they mainly try to recover through donations.

Sponsors/Donors

The Banyan has three main sources of funding: funding agencies (a combination of Indian and a very few international agencies), government grants and revenues from events. Whereas the government provides 8–12 per cent of funding, about 32 per cent of the budget is donated by funding agencies like the Sir Ratan Tata Trust or Zürich Financial. In addition, there is a small group of individual donors which regularly contribute.

Apart from the fundraising events, it also receives a lot of small, non-monetary contributions in the form of, clothing, food, medicine and the like. Other sources are the donations from several companies and donations through their website.

Networking

The Banyan has a database of 75 partners and a dedicated person within The Banyan is responsible to inform, integrate and support them. The Banyan believes that synergies between organizations are crucial for their own success. Furthermore The Banyan is part of two larger networks, the National Association for Mentally Ill (http://namiindia.in/book5.htm) and the South Asian Advocacy Network. As The Banyan strives to replicate its model throughout other parts of India, the organization also has several partner NGOs which are interested in bringing The Banyan's work forward. To do this, The Banyan offers the partner NGOs capacity building programmes for replication of the model by providing training, visiting them and then enabling them to distribute The Banyan's services through their own network. Another form of linking with partners relates to more general topics such as mental illness or the problems of marginalized people and then addressing the government and advocating for these issues. Together with the Institute of Mental Health and the Chennai city policy, The Banyan has founded the helpline 'Dial 100' to ensure homeless, mentally-ill women and men fast access to support and care.[2] Apart from the helpline, The Banyan trains police personnel about the specifics of this group.

Research

The Banyan Academy of Leadership and Management (BALM) is the education and research arm of The Banyan, which has been founded as an independent entity to build leadership capabilities in the development sector. The BALM, aims at providing the desperately needed linkage between theory and practice in the development sector. Their key objectives are:

1. Create the next generation of leaders in the development sector who will think, initiate and implement to promote equity.
2. Bridge the divide between practice and knowledge.

3. Raise the bar on quality of services in the development sector through interventions initiated by effective professionals and managers.
4. Lead advocacy initiatives.

The short-term approach concentrates on workshops for those already working in the field. This enhances the everyday duties through best practices case studies and thus promotes the so-called Banyan DNA, the main idea behind the NGO. In one of its long-term approaches, BALM works closely together with the Institute for Financial Management and Research (IFMR), which offers a two-year MBA, in cooperation with the BALM, to educate the leaders for the future.

The BALM has signed an MoU with the University College London (UCL) for collaboration in offering short-term courses for professionals in the development sector. Plans are also on the anvil to offer a Masters course which would combine the academic rigour of theoretical frameworks offered by UCL with the experiential learning offered by The Banyan and its partner NGOs.

Currently, a number of research projects are underway to build capabilities and knowledge in the field of mental illness and homelessness.

Communication Strategies

Main External Communication Channels

The Banyan strives for continuous contact with volunteers, donors and all people that are committed to the organization. They consider direct, personal contact as the most effective communication channel which they try to combine with a visit to the NGO. The annual report lists all initiatives, events as well as achievements and financial information. In addition to this, other communication channels include workshops, BALM, posters, speeches, brochures, newsletters (internal and external), visits to schools and colleges, direct mailings, media and press releases and so on. To engage the donors and other interested people, The Banyan-blog has been set up to encourage the dialogue between the organization and its supporters. On its official website, the NGO operates a kind of global news station called 'The Hub', which allows interested people to gain as much information about current happenings related not only to the organization itself, but also to issues related to its work. The links provided for further reading cover the latest findings in research related to mental disorders, other important news concerned with the changing events in the development sector and science-related information regarding new drugs or treatment for illnesses such as Alzheimer's disease or schizophrenia.

Internal Communication Channels

Apart from emails and SMS messages, regular meetings take place during the week with different departments, where each programme is reviewed by the other senior coordinators. Once in a month there is a review meeting, and every three months an event calendar meeting. All the weekly meetings are recorded and archived for future reference. In addition, project groups summarize their activities and outcomes monthly. The report is then sent via email to The Banyan staff and to some critical stakeholders.

Research on the Communication

The Banyan researches outcomes of their communication efforts, but in a very informal and unstructured way. From time to time a group of Banyan staff reviews the success of the communication efforts.

Campaigns

The organization predominantly implements permanent campaigns, including those which create awareness in rural areas, those targeting students, and others which are focused on government officials. In some cases the NGO is invited by official institutions, while in other cases, when no official invitation is extended, it develops its own education strategy.

In keeping with its focus on spreading awareness about issues of mental health, its treatment and cure, it has started conducting street theatre, which hase been very successful. It is dramatic, entertaining and effective in reaching out to a significant number of people in rural communities simultaneously.

Other types of campaigns focus on promoting The Banyan's model in other states, although this is related more to advocacy and long-term strategy. To achieve that, twice a year two different workshops take place, involving 75 to 100 key stakeholders across the country per event. As the latter is very closely related to its marketing efforts, all the communication channels and marketing tools discussed further, slide into this category.

Evaluation of Campaigns

The Banyan measures the success of its campaigns through surveys, sending a review form before and after campaigning. The inclusion of items like sensitivity and participation gives an indication regarding the awareness levels prior to and following the campaign, although the performance indicators for evaluation depend on the type of campaign.

Advertising and Marketing Strategies

A lot of the Banyan's marketing is linked to its spirit.

Vandana Gopikumar

The Banyan's marketing tools have evolved over time. Initially, the operative work was brought to the fore and stakeholders were mainly a very close group of friends, but with size and changing needs the organization has adapted and professionalized the marketing efforts and started to incorporate mass media as a very effective channel. Also, they continually make 'cold calls' to market their organization. They also place huge bets on their media presence: they engage journalists and editors to write about the organization to make stakeholders feel passionate about The Banyan. Furthermore the organization has been able to attract well known, highly regarded individuals and organizations as sponsors for The Banyan's work and to help spread the word. Those sponsors and ambassadors come from various spheres of public life: celebrities such as actors, directors, politicians or people who run fashion shows. Most of the interaction with these people serves various purposes such as the marketing the cause and in getting mental illness discussed; thereby spreading the message all over the country, especially in the rural areas, where people do not have much awareness about mental illness. Besides this, the other purpose of having ambassadors is fundraising.

During the last few years there has been a change in strategy as now almost all the marketing tools are tilted towards advocacy.

Advocacy at all levels, along with expansion of projects, has thus become the key focus at The Banyan. Advocacy is being mainly done to create awareness and public demand for mental health services.

Advocacy at The Banyan is carried out at three levels:

1. Working with clients and care givers to create awareness on mental health issues and to create a lobby for mental health.
2. Working with the government and promote public–private partnerships to find solution to mental health issues.
3. Creating public awareness through various forms of social marketing and to create agents for social change with regard to mental health.

Contact

55/18, Vinobaji Street
Opposite Kamaraj 4th Street
Gandhi Salai
Choolaimedu
Chennai – 94.
Phone: 91-44-42233666, 42233600, 26530504.
Website: http://www.thebanyan.org

Notes

1. Vandana Gopikumar and Vaishnavi Jayakumar in a personal interview with Svenja Falk, April 2007.
2. Men, however, are not submitted to The Banyan. They are referred to other institutions.

Evaluation and Policy Change

THE SECTION looks at how to maintain consistent evaluation. Questions to be answered are:

1. Have I reached my strategic objectives?
2. Can my communication strategy be considered successful?

The tools introduced for doing this are evaluation and media tracking.

EVALUATION

Have strategic goals been achieved? One can easily answer this question with an unequivocal 'yes' if policy change is initiated and the state and the community are starting to look differently at the question of children with HIV/AIDS. However, to ensure organizational learning, it makes a lot of sense to look at the milestones defined in the work plan. To understand where you could become even better, you need to look at the different research, analysis and social aspects of your project. There are a number of options for checking the impact that you have made:

1. Survey your Key Stakeholders
   You might use survey techniques to get your stakeholders view on your performance. What have they perceived as best

practice, and where they have diagnosed glitches? To achieve the best out of this, use a non-standardized questionnaire with open questions. Ideally, your survey will try to include representatives from communities, public administration, politics, academia, media, the business world and other NGOs.

2. Revisit your Milestones
   Which milestones have been achieved on time and on budget? Where did you face delays or overspending and what were the reasons? Did you stick to our original strategy or did you change the direction? From this evaluation, you should summarize your results to make them accessible for your team and, potentially, partner NGOs and stakeholders.

3. Assess the Outcomes
   Can the strategy implementation and your political communication approach be considered successful? Remember, one of your main objectives was to ensure that society and policy-makers look at the issues of children with HIV/AIDS jointly. You can check this by interviewing decision makers, testing the unaided awareness of this link. This basically implies that the decision makers bring the issues up themselves without any hints provided by you.

MEDIA TRACKING

> *Wind puffs up empty bladders, opinions, fools...*
>
> Socrates

To obtain a view on how your campaign has been perceived, a powerful tool at your disposal is media tracking. First and foremost, you count the number of articles in the print media. It is important to assess who has actually written about your organization, and it helps to group the media according to its relevance in the general public. You should group them by relevance to see where you have made the most impact. Moreover, one must not forget to check the internet. A very insightful reference is the readers' comment section.

Apart from the quantitative aspect, the qualitative aspect is very important: the framing of the content, which is to say the context within which it is represented. You can review below the definition and the examples presented by the Communication Consortiums Media Center (2004, 17) and targeted at NGOs:

> The way issues are packaged—by means of carefully designed words and phrases, visual clues, and selection of symbolic communicators—affects how the public thinks about those issues. Framing influences the perception and interpretation of media consumers and politicians alike. The power of framing can be seen in the way the following competing phrases set up the debate of a controversial social practice. 'Is it energy conservation' or 'energy efficiency'?

Also, what is the context within which your campaign is portrayed and who are the people quoted? What is the underlying tone of the article? The results of your media tracking and evaluation can become the foundation for a more in-depth analysis of the quality of your media exposure.

POCA's three way political communication channel has been successful, they are heard when their respective policy field is discussed. Apart from expert arenas they are also in the media where they have been able to be present as the central voice on this issue.

POLICY CHANGE

> *Never doubt that a small group of thoughtful, committed citizens can change the world. Indeed, it is the only thing that ever has.*

Margaret Mead

Public policy is a combination of goals, laws, rules and funding priorities set by public officials and decision-makers and it determines how government meets needs, solves problems and spends public funds. It is established by law (legislative), regulated by government agencies (executive) and monitored by the court system (judicial). As discussed by Avner (2004) the arenas of influence where public policy is decided are:

1. The legislature (Congress)
2. The court system (Supreme Court)
3. Regulatory agencies (Department of Education)
4. The media
5. Public opinion

Actually achieving policy change, however, is not necessarily the end as governments can choose to ignore policies or renege on them. Therefore, NGOs often have to push the judiciary to enforce existing laws or pressure public administration decision-makers to allocate budgets differently in order to actually make sure the changes occur. Typically, this process is an ongoing one and perhaps a never-ending journey.

To help achieve policy change, Chapman and Fisher (2000) have put a number of helpful prerequisites on the international, national and local level (see Table 11.1). These prerequisites, in combination with doing your homework regarding strategic research, strategy formulation and political communication should position you well to develop and achieve a different approach to communities, municipalities, governments, and educational and health institutions in order to better tackle the problem you have been addressing.

So in our specific case, you have successfully initiated a policy change in the way society and the government handles the issue, if:

1. You have increased awareness of the key decision-makers that the issues of HIV/AIDS and youth health cannot be treated separately.
2. You have increased the budget allocation by government to provide specific programmes addressing the needs of this specific group through educational and health infrastructure.
3. You have identified that the media is picking up on this topic through more coverage in television documentaries and in newspaper and magazine articles.

TABLE 11.1
Resources for Policy Change

Level	Arenas	What is Particularly Helpful?
International	International NGOs	Existence of International codes, Legislation and Convention
	Multilateral organizations	Active international campaign
	National governments	Consumer activism
	Consuming public	
	Voting public	
	Industry	
National/regional	National government	Progressive legislation, upholding rights
	Regional government	Legal pressure points
	Judiciary	(e.g. Supreme Court)
	Public opinion	History of social activism and NGO activity
	National NGOs	Aware population,
	Industry	labelling systems and interdependent monitoring
Grassroots	Communities	Active civil-society organizations
	Grassroot NGOs	Aware population
	Families	Active individuals
	Individuals	

Source: Chapman and Fisher (2000).

Conclusion

Strategic planning and political communication are the prerequisites for successfully initiating policy change. This applies to NGOs in the same way as it does to political parties, associations, interest groups or corporations. Getting the attention of decision-makers and urging them to change the way governments or societies do things has become quite a challenge. Even if you have a well thought strategy, your overall objectives still may not be achieved. Thus, it is paramount that you differentiate an NGO by the services it provides, the way it positions itself and the method by which it communicates its objectives. Competition for resources and public attention is stiff and depending on the economic conditions at the time, these could become even scarcer. Many policy-makers and economic experts expect the volatility of markets to continue, so you need to be quick while still maintaining reasonable caution. To be positioned for success, there are some basic, easy-to-follow rules you need to have:

1. Take people along – this is the most important success factor. Without support of key stakeholders nothing will happen.
2. Do not try to do everything at the same time – make sure you do not become swamped by immediately jumping on every new idea or opportunity presented to you. It is better to focus on getting a few things right rather than indiscriminately multi-tasking and winding up with half-baked results.
3. Get the basics right – passion and conviction about what you are doing is great, but make sure you do excellent, fact-based research to support your argument.
4. Have a clear view of who your most relevant stakeholders are – it is important to hook-up with the right people that will accompany you on your journey.
5. Make sure you are representing the interests of the people you are fighting for – do not make them an object of your initiatives but rather serve as a facilitator so that they can pursue their interests.

References

Anheier, H., M. Glasius and Mary Kaldor (eds). 2004. *Global Civil Society 2004/5.* London: Sage Publications.

Asian Philanthropy Consortium. 2003. *India.* Quezon City. Available online at: http://www.asiapacificphilanthropy.org/node/19 (Accessed on 21 March 2008).

——. 2007. *Philanthropy and Law in South Asia: Recent Developments in Bangladesh, India, Nepal, Pakistan and Sri Lanka.* Quezon City. Available online at: http://www.asiapacificphilanthropy.org/files/PALISA%20Update%20Works hop%20Report%20September%202007.pdf (Accessed on 4 April 2008).

Avner, M. 2004. *The Nonprofit Board Member's Guide to Lobbying and Advocacy.* Saint Paul: Fieldstone Alliance.

Baringhorst, S. 1998. 'Zur Mediatisierung des politischen Protests: Von der Institutionen-zur "Greenpeace-Demokratie"?' in U. Sarcinelli (ed.), *Politikvermittlung und Demokratie in der Mediengesellschaft,* pp. 326–44. Bonn: Bundeszentrale für politische Bildung 1998 and Opladen: Westdeutscher Verlag.

Bonk, K., H. Griggs and E. Tyne. 1999. *The Jossey-Bass Guide to Strategic Communications for Nonprofits: A Step-by-Step Guide to Working with the Media to Generate Publicity, Enhance Fundraising, Build Membership, Change Public Policy, Handle Crises, and More!* Jossey-Bass.

Brie, M., and H. Pietzker. 2004. 'NGOs in China', WZB Discussion Paper, Berlin. Available online at: http://bibliothek.wzb.eu/pdf/2004/iii04-110.pdf (Accessed on 17 April 2009).

Cabanero-Verzosa, C. 2003. *Strategic Communication for Development Projects.* Washington: The World Bank.

Chapman, J., and T. Fisher. 2000. 'The Effectiveness of NGO Campaigning: Lessons from the Practice', *Development in Practice,* 10(2): 151–65.

Communication Consortium Media Center. 2004. *Guidelines for Evaluating Nonprofit Communications Efforts.* Washington. Available online at: http://www mediaevaluationproject.org/Paper5.pdf (Accessed on 4 April 2008).

Cooperrider, D., and W. Pasmore. 1991. 'The Organization Dimension of Global Change', *Voluntas*, 44(8): 1037–55.

Gordenker, L., and T. Weiss. 1996. 'Pluralizing Global Governance: Analytical Approaches and Dimensions', in L. Gordenker and T. Weiss (eds), *NGOs, the UN, and Global Governance*, pp. 17–51. Boulder, CO: Lynne Rienner Publishers.

Gray, R. 2006. *Anti-Whaling Campaign in Australia*. Queensland: The Change Agency.

Farrell, D., and P. Webb. 2000. 'Political Parties as Campaign Organizations', in R. Dalton and M. Wattenberg (eds), *Parties Without Partisans: Political Change in Advanced Industrial Democracies*. Oxford: Oxford University Press.

Furtak, F. 1997. *Nichtstaatliche Akteure in den internationalen Beziehungen: NGOs in der Weltpolitik*. München: Tuduv.

Hallin, D. C., and P. Mancini. 2004. *Comparing Media Systems: Three Models of Media and Politics*. Cambridge: Cambridge University Press.

Hamel, G., and C. K. Prahalad. 1989. 'Strategic Intent', *Harvard Business Review*, 67(May–June): 63–76.

Heins, V. 2002. *Weltbürger und Lokalpatrioten. Eine Einführung in das Thema Nichtregierungsorganisationen*. Opladen: Leske and Budrich.

Hovland, I. 2005. *Successful Communication: A Toolkit for Researchers and Civil Society Organizations*. London: Overseas Development Institute.

Hovland, I. and D. Start. 2004. *Tools for Policy Impact: A Handbook for Researchers*. London: Overseas Development Institute.

Keck, M. E., and K. Sikkink. 1998. *Activists Beyond Borders. Transnational Advocacy Networks in International Politics*. New York: Cornell University Press.

Kunz, Johannes. Unpublished. *Strategiefindung von Non-Profit-Organisationen*. PhD thesis submitted to University St. Gallen in 2006. Available online at: http://www.unisg.ch/www/edis.nsf/wwwDisplayIdentifier/3136/$FILE/dis3136.pdf (Accessed on 17 April 2009).

Lijphart, A. 1971. 'Comparative Politics and the Comparative Method', *American Political Science Review*, 65(3): 682–93.

Minto, B. 1996. *The Minto Principle*. London: Minto Books International.

Nathan, D., D. N. Reddy and G. Kelkar. 2008. *International Trade and Global Civil Society*. New Dehli: Routledge.

Nadesan, Majia Holmer. 2001. 'Post-Fordism, Political Economy, and Critical Organizational Communication Studies', *Management Communication Quarterly*, 15 (2, November): 259–67.

Negrine, R., and S. Papathanassoppoulos 1996. 'The "Americanization" of Political Communication', *The Harvard International Journal of Press/Politics*, 1(2): 45–62.

Norris, P. 2000. *A Virtuous Circle: Political Communications in Post-Industrial Societies*. New York: Cambridge University Press.

Ostrower, F. 1995. *Why the Wealthy Give. The Culture of Elite Philanthropy*. New Jersey: Princeton University Press.

Pitt, C., C. Loehr and A. Malviya. 2005. *Campaigns, Evidence and Policy Influence: Lessons from International NGOs*. Odi. Available online at: http://www.odi.org.uk/Rapid/Projects/postgrad/docs/Project3_Campaigns.pdf (Accessed on 6 March 2008).

Porter, Michael E. 1980. *Competitive Strategy*. New York: The free Press, Macmillan Publishing.

——. 2008. 'The Five Competitive Forces that Shape Strategy', *Harvard Business Review*, 86(1): 78–93.

Participatory Research in Asia (PRIA). 2002. *The NON Profit Sector in India*. Delhi: PRIA.

Reid, E. (ed.). 2000. *Nonprofit Advocacy and the Policy Process*, volume 1. Washington: The Urban Institute.

Römmele, A., and R. Gibson. 2001. 'A Party-Centred Theory of Professionalized Campaigning', *The Harvard International Journal of Press/Politics*, 6(4), 31–43.

Room to Read. 2008. *Annual Report*. Room to Read.

Salamon, L. M., and H. K. Anheier. 1997. *Defining the Nonprofit Sector*. Manchester: Manchester University Press.

Salomon, L., S. Wojciech Sokolowski and Regina List. 2003. *Global Civil Society: An Overview*. Baltimore: Center for Civil Society Studies, John Hopkins University. Available online at: http://www.jhu.edu/ccss/publications/pdf/globalciv.pdf (Accessed on 17 April 2009).

Salzmann, J. 1998. *Making the News: A Guide for Nonprofits and Activists*. Boulder: Westview Publications.

Smucker, B. 1999. *The Nonprofit Lobbying Guide*. Washington: Independent Sector.

Sooryamoorthy, R. and K. D. Gangrade. 2006. *NGOs in India. A Cross-Sectional Study*. Jaipur: Rawat.

Take, Ingo. 2000. 'Transnationale Allianzen als Antwort auf die Herausforderungen des 21. Jahrhunderts', *Forschungsjournal Neue Soziale Bewegungen*, 13(1): 87–91.

Thomaß, B. 2007. *Mediensysteme im internationalen Vergleich*. Konstanz: UVK Verlagsgesellschaft.

Tilly, C. 2004. *Social Movements, 1768–2004*. Boulder, Colorado: Paradigm Publishers.

Time Magazine, 19 May 2008, p. 25.

Transition Monitoring Group. 2006. *A Handbook For NGOs: On Advocacy & Lobbying Skills To Promote Electoral Reforms*. Available online at http://www.tmgnigeria.org/publications/mannualonadvocacy-lobbying.pdf (Accessed on 23 May 2008).

Union of International Association. 2007. *Yearbook of International Organizations*. Munich: K. G. Saur Verlag.

Voss, K. 2007. *Öffentlichkeitsarbeit von Nichtregierungsorganisationen.* Wiesbaden: Verlag für Sozialwissenschaften.

Weisskopf, Michael. 2008. 'Obama: How He Learned to Win', *Time Magazine*, 19 May, p. 2.

World Bank. 2006. *Inclusive Growth and Service Delivery: Building on India's Success.* Available online at: http://siteresources.worldbank.org/SOUTHASIAEXT/ Resources/DPR_FullReport.pdf (Accessed on 5 June 2008).

Yin, R. K. 1984. *Case Study Research – Design and Methods.* London: Sage Publications.

About the Authors

Accenture-Stiftung, Germany was instituted by the management consulting, technology services and outsourcing company Accenture with a mission to strengthen Accenture's social and scientific commitment in Germany. Accenture-Stiftung believes that companies have a responsibility to engage proactively with the communities in which they live and work. Its mission is to support communities in need as well as help to improve access to and quality of education.

School of Communication Management, International University in Germany, Bruchsal is an interdisciplinary enterprise of high repute. It offers two programmes, Bachelors in International Communication Management and Masters in Political Management— both programmes link academic excellence with applied learning. The school trains young communication professionals as well as young leaders in politics to meet contemporary global challenges. It also collaborates with scholars in the UK, the US and Sweden on campaign communication strategy and is home to *The Journal for Political Consulting and Policy Advice*. Professor Dr Andrea Römmele is Dean and Programme Director of the School of Communication Management.

The Banyan, India was founded in 1993, when it started off as a shelter and transit home for homeless women with mental illness who had wandered from their homes across the country and ended up on the streets of Chennai. In its 15 years of operation, The Banyan has responded to the needs of over 2,000 women and reunited over 1,100 women with their families. As an NGO working on rescue, treatment and rehabilitation of mentally ill women, The Banyan has evolved from a non-profit organization to a for-impact organization with its strategic interventions, modes of operation, systems of treatment and care, community outreach and research. Its mission is to address the rights and the needs of the completely marginalized and act as a catalyst to raise awareness and acceptance of a range of issues, and to create the momentum for government and society to develop appropriate legal and social responses.